AFENI SHAKUR

EVOLUTION OF A REVOLUTIONARY

AFENI SHAKUR

EVOLUTION

OF A

REVOLUTIONARY

Jasmine Guy

ATRIA BOOKS

New York London Toronto Sydney

ATRIA BOOKS
1230 Avenue of the Americas
New York, NY 10020

ISBN: 0-7434-7053-2

First Atria Books hardcover edition February 2004

Permissions can be found on page 225

10 9 8 7 6 5 4 3 2 1

ATRIA BOOKS is a trademark of Simon & Schuster, Inc.

Manufactured in the United States of America

Designed by Jaime Putorti

For information regarding special discounts for bulk purchases,
please contact Simon & Schuster Special Sales at 1-800-456-6798
or business@simonandschuster.com

This book is dedicated to Tupac Amaru Shakur

ACKNOWLEDGMENTS

My Guy Family: One of my greatest gifts is that I was born into this tribe. My mother, Jaye Rudolph, who taught me how to write, fed my talent, and grounded my work; my father, William V. Guy who did not lie to me and gave clear, objective criticism; and my sister, Monica Guy, whose journalistic background and creative brilliance compensated for my lacking.

My Duckette Family: Thank you Mitch and Imani for allowing me time away from you to do this book; Mama Lorine and Tracie, for loving me as a daughter and a sister.

My Circle: Gi Gi, Monica, Tambre, Kyme, Gina, and Dianne.

My Friends: Fatima, Jada, Adriana, and Susan.

My Publisher/Editor: Judith Curr and Luke Dempsey.

My Fortress: Karolyn Ali, who believed from the beginning that this would be done and saw to it that it was.

My Shakur Sisters: Sekyiwa, Glo, Jamala, and, of course, Afeni.

Preface

The purpose of a preface has always eluded me. I do not read introductions, prefaces, or any words that precipitate the author's. I feel the writer's words are the first and last I should read. I've been asked to write a preface, a beginning to the beginning, a prebeginning as it were. So, I write this reluctantly but dutifully in case I may be wrong about what you may understand or not understand in this book.

Let me begin by saying that my life has been empowered by the strength of black women. I am not solely empowered by *black* women or black *women* but in reality I listen most immediately to their struggle. It is their message that helps me beat down my personal demons. African-American women are vulnerable. They hurt. They fear. Yet, they spit in the face of degradation, racism, and poverty. They fight for freedom in their own personal ways. They create babies and they nurture them. They make love to their men and they love them. They laugh and sing and dance. They are not crybabies. So, it is no wonder that once I knew the story of Afeni Shakur, I wanted her story told.

Over time, over heartache, over joy, over loss, over birth, and over death, our friendship was born. With Afeni I've experienced a decade of lessons, love, loyalty, and truth. With Afeni I have a decade of friendship and a decade of learning a friend.

In this book I share the personal conversations Afeni and I have had over the course of our friendship so that you might get to know her as I know her . . . intimately.

Though she is complex and fascinating, make no mistake: The purpose of this book is not to titillate. As Afeni told me pointedly and firmly, she is not interested in being fascinating.

"I want to reach people who have big problems," she told me, "People that look like they won't get through. I want to talk about how you get through garbage . . . just putting one foot in front of the other. I want to talk about how you can survive without destroying yourself in the process and that when you do survive there's something left . . . some spirit left for the next day."

Afeni looked at me hard at that moment and asked me one good time, "You think we could do that?"

I smiled when I said, "Yes. Afeni, with your story we can do that . . . for somebody."

—JASMINE GUY

ONE

The Stuff

"It's important to know the stuff you came from."
—AFENI SHAKUR

I travel east on I-20 as the sun sets behind me, passing exits I no longer recognize. Old fears of being lost on the highway in Stone Mountain, Georgia, resurface, even though I'm told it's no longer the crackerland of my childhood. Black folk live out here now, far beyond the parameters of my youth. Today, Atlanta stretches past Cumberland Mall, Six Flags, and even Stone Mountain. Things have changed and I missed the transition. I feel strangely stuck right in the middle of my life. There was a time when my life was *all* ahead of me. Today, there is a big chunk behind me and maybe just as much in front. All this means is, I still have time to change my attitudes and sensibilities, but I am just less inclined to do so.

Let's say I'm just a little less flexible. Like an uncle of mine who still says "colored" instead of "black." He just never got used to saying "Black" or "Negro," and didn't understand what difference it made or why he had to make a change. The change was irrelevant to him . . . "African-American" was out of the question.

So, the irony of the famed revolutionary and impassioned mother of a rapper—superstar Tupac Shakur—now residing in suburban, once-Klan-country Georgia is not lost on me. In fact, I have learned to expect the unexpected from Afeni Shakur. Not because she means to be complex or contradictory, but because she just is. That is her truth, and it's a truth that fascinates me. I've grown to love my friend Afeni.

As I drive I think back to December 1, 1994, the day I met Afeni. At the time, I was writing a screenplay about a fictitious young woman in the '60s who was raising her daughter while still living with her own mother. The piece was, or still is if I ever get finished writing it, a three-generation piece about Black women. The young woman in the middle is a fictitious, composite character of Angela Davis and Afeni Shakur. My plan was to meet Afeni and hopefully have her help me develop this particular character and perhaps give me her insights on the other two.

The way I met her was not how I'd imagined, though. In fact, I was thrust into a tumultuous family trauma her son, my friend, Tupac, had been brutally shot five times in the foyer of a New York recording studio on a Sunday night; had left Bellevue Hospital on a Monday, and was in court on a Tuesday morning for a sexual assault hearing. So, on December 1, 1994, I was early for the court hearing and waiting in a vast hallway with Jada Pinkett, a close friend of mine and an even closer friend to Tupac Shakur. We were waiting to get a glimpse of Tupac on his way into court and let him know we were near and there for him. At that time, I didn't even know the charges or the circumstances of the trial. I just knew that Tupac was shot the night before in the entrance of the recording studio, and I needed to be there to support my friends—Jada and Tupac.

The crazy events of the last two days had me reeling, but I tried to consciously stay in the moment. *It is Tuesday morning. Tuesday morning. You're in New York. You're at the courthouse.* I remember talking myself into the present moment of that day, but I kept slipping out. *Tupac is shot. Someone shot Tupac.* Today is Tuesday morning . . . *Five times! Who did it? He's at Bellevue. . . .* That was Monday, which would be yesterday. . . . *He's out. Tupac's gone. He left. The hospital? He didn't feel safe up in there. At Bellevue? Monday, that was yesterday. Where is he? I don't know, but I'm going to New York.* Here I am Tuesday morning at the courthouse. *Just be here. Just be present. Someone may need you.*

And that's where I was—jumping back and forth in my head—this Monday, the day I first saw Afeni Shakur. A tight group clustered at the end of the hall, surrounding a wheelchair holding an ashen, bandaged, diminutive

Tupac. Two women headed the clan that hovered over him, and I later learned that his family was indeed a "clan." At the time, however, it just looked to me like a bunch of *folk*. I mistook the lady in charge to be Afeni at first notice, but the lady was Glo, Afeni's sister. Afeni stood beside her. Glo was stern and serious, as I had imagined Afeni would be, and Glo checked me out when she first saw me, like I was some little wannabee trying to get next to Tupac. Afeni, on the other hand, was warmer. She embraced me like I was an old friend. Little did I know I would grow to be just that— an old friend.

I sit with this memory of December 1994 when I first met Afeni. I sit with this memory now in Stone Mountain, Georgia, as I approach the long driveway of Afeni's house— the house Tupac bought for her. Eight years later, I get to sit with my Afeni, and I relish my time alone in her world. She wants to talk of origins, beginnings. She is ready now to reveal her own history. She is ready now because she's taken some time with herself to reflect on her life. She needed this time because her beloved son died. He didn't die the first time he was shot five times in the foyer of the New York recording studio, but he was shot again two years later in Las Vegas. And this time, she lost him. September 13, 1996. So, Afeni needed some time to look at her life and work out why she is still here. Now, she wants to tell *her* story, and she called me to tell it to. She says she's been back to her home and has spent some time with her people. She understands more about her mama, her daddy, and their mamas and daddies. She's had some time to go back home to Lumberton, North Carolina, and Norfolk, Virginia, and revisit where her life began as Alice Faye Williams.

Her house is set back from the street. I park next to a few cars in the driveway, and I recognize one of them as Tupac's prized Mercedes. I smile and walk up the steps to Afeni's front door. It is ajar, so, I just step in and yell a few "hellos."

"I'm in the back," Afeni calls.

I follow her voice through the airy living room and wood-paneled den. On the walls are powerful oil portraits of Tupac. The photos on the mantel above the brick fireplace celebrate Afeni's babies, her grandchildren, nieces, nephews, grandnieces, grandnephews, and the offspring of her ex-comrades and their children's children. A generation has passed since the revolution. My baby, Imani, is up there too. And I realize I am part of this family as well, and I'm grateful for the inclusion.

I reach Afeni's bedroom only to find her backlit in the doorway of her veranda, her silhouetted arms reaching out to me. I get closer and I see her glistening eyes smile broadly. She hugs me, strong and hearty, as if she were a big ole man instead of the small-boned little lady she is. I enjoy Afeni's hug. It carries weight and time and the sense that it may be the last one. So I hold on tight. There aren't many people in my life this happy to see me and she always is.

"Afeni," I say. "I can't believe your house. It's so warm and inviting and—"

"I got furniture," she proclaims.

We laugh and I add, "I didn't crawl over lumps of sleeping teenagers on the floor either. And it's light in here. And clear."

"Yeah," Afeni says. "I only smoke back here now, in my room and on my porch. 'Cause of the kids, you know."

"It's lovely, Fe. I'm proud of you." Having a house that is a home is a major accomplishment for Afeni, who has spent most of her adult life an impoverished gypsy. In dire straits she always stayed with her sister Glo, and dire straits were frequent.

"Come on out here." Afeni leads the way. "Come on out here on my porch."

The porch is deep and long, and wraps around the house like a huge knitted scarf. In one corner, Afeni's chaise lounge sits to the right of a small table. Another cushioned chair to the left of the small table faces the sprawling pine forest of her backyard. In the farthest corner a large color TV flickers, on mute, but full of CNN.

"Shit, you might as well move the bed out here, too," I exclaim. I've never seen a TV on an outdoor porch before. I nestle in my chair and let the warm, rich Georgia air rest on my face. God, I miss humidity.

"This is all I ever wanted," Afeni says. "This right here? This is the best thing Tupac ever did for me."

"It is nice, Afeni, and very peaceful." I began to see why she's in Stone Mountain.

"Land. We always wanted land. Shit, I come from share-croppers. Of course, they wanted land, too. They understood the value of *owning* your own land, 'cause they never owned nothing. My great-grandmother, Millie Ann, she was the last person in our family to have land, and it has taken all this time for us to own land again Now, Black people want trinkets, cars and clothes, and shit. That's part of the genocide, the loss of values. It is killing us, as a people."

Afeni shakes her head. "Millie Ann had land, and she lost it. Her sons got busted, and she put the house up for bail. Then it burned down. Black people had land, you know, but we lost it. It was hard to keep it, though, but when that land got taken, it broke us down a little more. So, the next time the children came up, they didn't know it is the *land* that is important. Now, they think the trinket is important 'cause their parents and their parents before them didn't own shit."

"And they died owning nothing," I add.

"And nothing to pass down," Afeni says.

"The Cadillac parked in front of unit B in the projects," I say to Afeni, the vision dear to me. Having grown up near a project in Atlanta, I get what she's saying about our skewed values.

"Exactly, but if you got your land, that's what you work for. I don't need no clothes, jewelry, and shit. Because now

I work to keep the land. I want a generator in case the electricity goes out. I want space so if someone needs a place to live, they can put a trailer up right there and have a home. I want my grandchildren to know how to garden and cultivate their own food. I want them to know because I come from farmers and people of the land and I lost it. You see that," Afeni points to a patch of dark soil with cabbage, lettuce, carrots thriving. "I tried to do that garden and I got calluses and shit. I burned my hands up! That shit is hard work. Them women in those days, my great-grandmother, my people, they worked their butts off from sunup to sundown to keep it up. You can't be spending your money on trinkets if you have to keep up your land."

I join in. "When I first got *A Different World* I bought a house. Actually, I did a Burger King commercial for sixty grand, and that was my down payment. Before I bought a nice car or a nice stereo system, I made sure I had a home that I owned."

Afeni taps my thigh. "Yes," she says excitedly. "Priority. And I'm glad your people taught you that. You knew early. It's taken me so many years to find my priority in life, only to come right back here where I began. Now, I know what I'm working for and striving for. The real estate man who showed me this place was happy to sell it to me, you know, until he found out who my son was. Then he wanted me to go and get a big ole fancy house."

"Yes, 'cause your son's a superstar! You need some marble and a fountain, some gates and some statues, a swimming pool!" I laugh because such showy opulence would be untrue to Afeni's real self.

"And I wanted the *land*, not the house. The land, to live on and to cultivate and pass on to my family."

Afeni inhales her Newport and surveys the deep forest green of her backyard. I notice new saplings planted on the edge of her small pine forest.

"Those new trees are what the babies planted," Afeni says proudly.

Afeni's "babies" are the Shakur family's next generation. The two sisters, Glo and Afeni, are at the helm—they are the keepers of the brood. Sekyiwa, Afeni's daughter, and Tupac's sister, has two children—Nzingha and Malik. Jamala, Glo's daughter, has one daughter—Imani. Katari, Glo's son, has a daughter as well, Kyira, the same name as my daughter. And on any given day, these cousins roam Afeni's yard, raid her refrigerator, and laugh up the rooms of her Stone Mountain refuge.

"Nzingha wanted a pine tree. So, that's her tree right there. That one is Imani's. And Leeki [Malik], he wanted a fruit-bearing tree. This one's his and look . . . there's some fruit! We plant a tree for Tupac on his birthday every year. Either here or on the farm."

Afeni also owns a 56-acre farm in Lumberton, North Carolina. She invites me to go there often, but I'm reluctant to travel too far from my double-tall, two-sugar-in-the-raw nonfat lattes.

"You got to come, Jasmine," Afeni insists. "Bring the

children. Children love it. I got cows and pigs. We grow our own vegetables—organic vegetables, without those chemicals and hormones that are killing our kids. We give away these clean vegetables to the people of Robeson County. They work the land, and they sell the produce. It's for them and by them." Afeni gets excited. "You see, Lumberton is the poorest county in North Carolina. Robeson County—the poorest. And what this means is . . ."

Afeni looks nothing like she did when I first met her in the halls of the courthouse doting over her bandaged son. Then, she was reticent, kind of caved in. She looked sad and tired, worried and scared. She was skinny then, too, maybe one hundred pounds and some change. Now, when I look at her beaming over her newly planted trees, her skin has some red in it, and her head is full of new thick hair—short and healthy without the patches of distress that once wore through.

"I've got some Lumbees helping me with my land," Afeni continues. "They come every day and work the land."

"What's a Lumbi?" I picture little gnomelike creatures with green skin and snakelike tails that only till the land at night.

"Lumbee's are Indians indigenous to that part of North Carolina."

"Lumbee. Never heard of them. But isn't that Cherokee country?"

"No, the Lumbee Indian came from the Sioux and

Cheraw. They mixed with some Spanish explorers early on. Then, you know, the English and Scottish came and they mixed with them, too. By that time, they started to lose their language and their customs and nobody knew what to call them. They were all mixed up."

"They spoke English?"

"Yes," Afeni is emphatic. "I'm telling you, they lost their culture and their language but they stayed separate. They knew they were Indians. They just needed a name. First they were Croatan Indians. Then they were Robeson County Indians. Then, the Cherokee of Robeson County. They've been called a lot of names. Lumbee came after a long fight to be recognized by the North Carolina legislature as a tribe. They named themselves after the Lumbee River."

Afeni takes a long drink of water, grabs her pack of Newports and continues. "I thought my great-grandmother married a Lumbee. Well, at least part Lumbee, part white dude, but he was just a white dude, really poor white trash."

"Was this your great-grandmother's second marriage?"

"No. This was her first."

"Then, this is your great-grandfather you're talking about. So, he's your grandmother's father," I reveal. "You act like he's no kin to you."

"Well," Afeni chuckles. "It's taken me a long time to deal with the fact that my great-grandmother married a white man. It will take a few more years to say he's my great-grandfather!"

"Damn, Afeni," I say. "You can't change the facts." But we are both laughing.

"But this is what I'm saying; I need to see things for what they are—always. And that's what I taught my kids to do." Afeni takes a breath. "And these were not nice white people this man came from. These were po' white trash people, like I said, and they disowned him for marrying my great-grandmother. . . . Tied him to a wagon and dragged him all the way through town."

"Some Jasper, Texas shit," I say, making reference to the recent torture killing of James Byrd.

"Not really, not like that, he wasn't *killed*. Because back then, kids played with wagons, draggin' each other around. So, it didn't kill you always, like what happened to James Byrd hooked up to that truck. This was more about humiliation, and him marrying my great-grandmother was humiliating to that white family. Even though they were po' white trash."

"Damn," I say, "Your great-grandmother married a white man in the twenties!"

"Earlier than that," Afeni responds. "My grandmother was born in 1899. So, her mama had to have gotten married before or around then."

"Deep." I'm surprised this couple made it through their marriage alive.

Afeni continues. "As a child, I'd tell people he was half Indian, 'cause my great-granddaddy being all white was too much for me to bear. I remember my great-grandmother. I have a picture of her in my house. Her and all her children. Half and half . . . like you." She nods at me. "But I said they were half Indian, at least till recently."

"What kind of Indian did you think they were?"

"Lumbee, probably . . ." Afeni says. "And that was cool with me because the Lumbee didn't take no shit from white folks. And sometimes Black folk would benefit from that. You know, them being in the middle was like a buffer. They did things we couldn't do as a group. They were unified and together. In fact, they ran the Klan out of Robeson County."

"Really?" I love to hear a good Klan-getting-their-ass-kicked story.

"Klan came in and tried to impose a ten o'clock curfew on the Indian and Black community. Posted notices up about race mixing and basically wanted to control the Lumbees and treat them like niggers. So, the Klan had a rally posted—the time and place and everything."

"Publicity."

"Wasn't no secret, and for weeks, we saw it coming."

"How old were you?" I ask.

"'Bout ten, I think. It was around my birthday, and the Klan had this rally near Maxton in some open field. Up until the day of that rally the Klan had been burning crosses and terrorizing folk in St. Paul's and were getting closer to Lumberton and Pembroke. They said they wanted to set the Indians straight, show 'em who's boss. Well, the Lumbees got guns and rifles and ambushed the Klan at their own rally. Folks say it was a mob scene. Shooting everywhere in the complete darkness of night. Black folk wanted to fight with them, but the Lumbees said they had it under control. They felt specifically challenged by the Klan, you know. They were like 'this is *our* battle.' So we all just waited to hear what went down in Maxton and rejoiced with the news that they ran the Klan out. Those white-hooded crackers ran into the woods like the little wing wangs they were." Afeni takes a drag and remembers. "That was a good day that mornin'. Miracle was nobody got killed."

"Was that your first smell of revolution?" I ask.

"That was my first taste of *resistance*. Resistance is what I felt. *Resist.* A sense of don't let that happen to you." Afeni looks at me to make sure I hear the difference. The difference between *revolt* and *resist.* "When Emmet Till was beaten and drowned the message was don't let that happen to you. Little girls raped in the cotton fields . . . Don't let that happen to you. White boy spit in my uncle's face . . . Don't let that happen to you. Woman's lip swollen, puffy and scarred . . . Don't let that happen to you. Resist. Not revolution. I didn't know shit about changing the world. I just knew there were some foul, hateful people in it that torture us for no reason, and I needed to resist that. Shit, that's all I knew. Because I was a little girl—six or seven years old—walking to school with my sister and a car full of grown-ass men would drive by, slow up and call us niggers and monkeys, and all I knew was I had to protect myself and resist."

"You learned quick. You learned early."

"Wasn't nothin' to learn. That's the way it was. That's what I saw."

"You learned white people could hate you so deeply they could kill. You learned what it was to be poor. Hated and poor."

"Let me say this . . ." Afeni sits up straight. "*Everybody* was poor. Nobody had shit. So, you don't feel poor when everybody's poor. You know, you aren't sticking out. That's not what they called me growing up—'po' this or 'po' that. It was more 'Nigger' this, 'Baldheaded' that, 'Skinny' this, and 'Tar baby' that. That's the kind of shit I got. But poor? We were all poor. In fact, that is what held us together as a community. Like our neighbor, Miss Hattie. This lady liked my mama, and she knew our situation. You didn't have to tell her anything or ask her anything, but this is how cool she was. She would wait for my daddy to leave because coming over there while he was home would have caused even more turmoil." Afeni looks ahead as if she can see Miss Hattie looking out her window. "And then she would just come over and take my mama grocery shopping. She'd take her to get groceries because she knew my dad didn't give her nothing for food. She would ask no questions, just take my mama shopping." Afeni seems amazed at the kindness of strangers. In spite of all the pain around her, life has sparkles of humanity. "My mother kept a calendar, and every Friday when my father got paid she would write down how much he gave her. So, she would know how much she had to work with for the week."

"Was it a set amount every week, like an allowance?"

"No, it fluctuated. One Friday, it was two dollars. Another Friday, it was six dollars. Another Friday, it was three—that's what he gave her."

"According to how much he made?"

"Shit, according to how much he *spent*." Afeni does a harrumph or a snort. The noise is hard to describe, but what it says is 'Baby, let me tell you.' "My daddy was a *street* nigga, and he was *loved* by the people in the streets. He understood the rules of the street, and when I say street, I'm talking Norfolk, Virginia, not New York streets. So when I say street, it's not the same street you know today. Here, you're basically talking about the difference between the people who were saved and sanctified and who went to church, versus the people who drank and didn't go to church. So, amongst those people—"

"Those drinkin', hangin' out on Saturday night people." I get it.

"Yeah, he was the bomb! The reason being he was an all right guy to these folks. He had principles, ethics, and he had a sense of himself. He was a small man, but unafraid. He was stubborn and arrogant. I get those qualities from my dad. The rebellion, the need to fight back and the need to be recognized as different."

"Uh-huh, and so did your son." It strikes me afresh that

they are so alike. It's a trip. "So you were close to your dad?"

"Well, you would think that I would be, but basically I resented him. I hated him around us. I hated him because he hurt my mom when he was home. My dad was a truck driver. He made deliveries. In between truck runs he would be home. He'd wait for us to go to school, and he'd start fighting with my mom and beating on her. My mama married to stay married, you know? That's all she knew. She was a *good* girl, and he treated her as if she were a person from the street. He married my mother, snatched her from Lumberton, her home, her family, everything familiar to her, and left her lost in the city. She was not equipped to be left alone in Norfolk, Virginia. She had always had her family! She was not used to being uncared for. She was never savvy, or slick, or hustlin' or none of that, and my dad tried to change her. That broke my mother and ultimately tore her down." Afeni seems hardened by the memory of her father.

"What broke her? Getting beat or being away from home?"

"All of it. The loss of her foundation. It ultimately led to her loss of faith so it all broke her down."

"What did she do?"

"I thought she was weak, because what I saw was her taking his shit. She wasn't a fighter, at least not a physical fighter. But one time in front of me and Glo my dad tried to hit her, and because we were there, my mother did not let that happen. We never saw that blow connect 'cause she threw hot grease on him. Right from the skillet she was holding. She never would have done that if she were alone with him. But we were standing right there, me and Glo, and she was protecting *us*. She didn't want her girls to see that hit, even though we knew it always went down like that. So, finally, one day we came home from school and my uncle Bob was there at the house. My mama always called her brother when my dad would hit her, but this time he took us back to Lumberton." Afeni tires of talking about this. She looks away from me, and her slender fingers search frantically for a loose dreadlock to tighten.

"Are you getting mad?" I ask her. "Is this a painful place go back to?"

She thinks, smokes and thinks. Way up, the tips of the pine trees bend in the breeze and she watches their ease. I notice her age today. Afeni looks fifty. Not because her skin has lost its smoothness; it has not. And not because drugs and cigarettes have tarnished her smile; they have not. She looks fifty today because she is comfortable today as she comes to terms with her past. This calm gives her grace and wisdom, and that's why she looks fifty. It's a beautiful thing to see.

"If I were gonna be angry about things, these are the things I would be angry about. These are the things I have been angry about. The things I lost because I did not have a father. I can't drive. I can't swim. I can't ride a bike, and I can't roller skate. Now, there's no reason I can't learn to do these things today. I could learn to do any of these things, but these are wounds that remain with me. I think I hold on to these *can'ts* on purpose. They are like my badge of injustice for a great injustice that has been done to me. Here I was . . . this bright little girl who wanted so much for her father to find her special and wonderful, and he never did. I mean he probably gave me the best he could give me, but that had nothing to do with what I needed. I needed a father who was there. I needed a father who was not a threat to my mom. . . .

"In Virginia, we lived upstairs, and in the back there were stairs that came up to our porch. The kitchen was where the back door was. Then there was a middle room that should've been a living room, but it was actually where me and Glo slept. The front room was my mom and dad's bedroom and the front porch came off of that. One day my sister was going up the back stairs in her skates and fell and broke her arm. My father was a very mean person, like his dad. He took away our skates and bikes, and we never had them again.

"So, there's another reason why I feel like I can't ride bikes or skate or drive a car. 'Cause all these things are locked into my father and what he didn't do for us. The reason I can't do those things is I've made prisons for myself. I got to dig my way out of these prisons, therapeutically, spiritually. For many people, driving is nothing. For me, it's like climbing a mountain. These are my hard things that I have to find it within myself to get over. I don't know that I will want to even if I'm able to."

"My mother didn't drive for a long time," I tell Afeni. "She had an accident before I was born and she didn't drive for ten or eleven years. To this day she won't drive on a highway, but she gets everywhere she needs to go on the surface streets. Shoot, I couldn't wait to drive."

"And I bet your daddy taught you," Afeni says.

"Yeah, he sure did. He taught me how to ride a bike, too. Brush my teeth without spattering Crest all over the chrome faucets, too." I know what she's saying.

Afeni continues: "That's why I understand my son so much. As a girl, I just hurt. I spent so much time searching for the cause of what was wrong with me in my parents; I could see what was fucked up about them. My mama was weak and sweet. My dad mean and arrogant. We were Black and poor in a place where that meant you weren't shit and I wasn't goin' down like that. So, I understand Tupac. He looked for the reasons in me just like I looked for the answers in my parents. When Tupac came at me with a bunch of motherfuckin' *whys*, I knew I had it coming."

"Did you ever find your reasons? Do you have any answers to your motherfuckin' *whys*?"

"Now I kinda get it." Afeni walks up to the railing. The sun melts into orange clouds, and the smell of fried chicken catches my attention. "My understanding of their lives doesn't make what they did right. But I accept what happened to my mom. I accept what happened to my dad, and acceptance is very important to me for my survival. I get them both as human beings, as two young people, with their circumstances. And I realize they did the best they could. I'm not mad at them for that. And that's good, because I've been mad a long time. For most of my life I've been angry."

The aroma of that chicken surrounds me and I turn my attention away from Afeni. For a second, it's like I'm dreaming, and the angel of sweet southern cooking has descended from the clouds.

A tall brown woman with a full face and smile stands in the doorway of Afeni's bedroom holding two steaming plates of fried chicken and sweet potatoes.

"Y'all want ice tea?" she asks walking toward us on the porch.

"What is this?" I exclaim, thrilled that my dream has come true. "I thought I was doin' the double-latte, blue plate special tonight." I chuck my cold, old Starbucks remains into the trash and clear the small table of my books, papers, cell phone, and shoulder bag.

"This is Mabel. She comes and cooks for me sometime, especially when the kids are coming over. I told her you'd be here today," Afeni says proudly.

"Miss Guy, I'm happy to meet you." Mabel extends her hand.

I begin to shake her hand, but then I give her a big hug. "It's so sweet of you to do this, Mabel. Thank you."

"Yes," Mabel beams. "Now try the cornbread and the greens 'fore they get cold."

"Miss Mabel, you just don't know. You just don't know how happy I am you've done this." I smile at Afeni because I know *she* knows. We dig in.

With drink and sustenance and the fresh Georgia air, Afeni is renewed. She tells me the tale of her parents' parents. As she lays out their story in even strokes I remember how reluctantly she used to tell her parents' story. Now, she recounts their stories as the natural order of life. It's as if she has made sense of her life by finding the sense in her people's lives. I listen intently, like I'm watching a good movie, but I never stop throwin' down Mabel's sweets and wings. God bless Mabel.

"The more I learn about who my people came from, the more I can accept who they turned out to be. Okay, here's my dad—Walter Williams Jr. My dad's father was Walter Williams Sr. His wife was Lena. Walter Sr. was about your height, five-two; Lena was about five-ten, maybe six feet. Now these are just the facts." I nod because I understand, but my mouth is too full to comment.

Afeni continues, "Now, Walter Sr. is a colored preacher with a small-man attitude. He and Lena had like fifteen children. They were all sharecroppers on a very large farm in North Carolina 'bout an hour out of Lumberton, closer to Virginia. Walter Sr. had a smoke-house, an orchard, watermelons, cantaloupes. He had cows, horses, and pigs. On Sunday the milk was milked from the cow in a big tub. I have memories of breakfast on his farm 'cause far as *I* knew, that was my *granddaddy's* farm. I didn't know sharecropping from ownership." Afeni sits back from her plate and gives her stomach room. She leans back but is not relaxed. I put my chicken bone down.

"Oh, Afeni," I say. "Breakfast and *my* grandpa. That is my most vivid memory of my grandfather. He would make a *huge* breakfast. And I'd eat anything. It was delicious. Grits. Bacon. Sausage. Eggs and brain."

"Eggs and brain," Afeni confirms. She knows what I'm talking about. "But a meaner man you've never seen than *my* grandfather." Afeni sees him plain as day. "Not in your whole life. He was cold, and that's how I see my daddy got fucked-up. When we visited my granddaddy, everybody could go and pick something out of his garden. I wanted a watermelon so bad. My grandfather said, 'You can't *have* a watermelon, but I will sell you one.' And I said, 'Fine,'" being the defiant little girl that I was. So, I went out into the farm and walked straight to the watermelon patch. I looked for a while at all the different watermelons and picked one just right. I was happy. I bring my watermelon to Walter Sr. I pay him his money and slice it open. Only to find out that the shit wasn't ripe. And he knew it, my grandfather, and he let me buy a fuckin' bad watermelon from his own goddamn farm." She blows the smoke out of her cigarette. "That's what I mean by *mean*, Jasmine. He wouldn't give me my money back, either, and that told me all that he was.

"He was cruel to his children, cruel to my dad, unfeeling, and this is the man my father came from. Now, unlike my mother's family, who tried to go to school but didn't quite know what to do with schooling once you got it, my dad's family knew what to do with an education. Even though these kids were working on the farm, they were all pushed by Preacher Daddy Walter Sr. to excel in school. My grand-daddy said his family 'wasn't no field nigger family.' The way out of being a field hand was to be a preacher or a teacher or something respectable like that. So, when my dad rejected my grandfather's calling to be a preacher, when he flat-out denied his father's wishes, he was forever outcast from the family. His mama, Lena, though she loved him, and my dad and brothers and sisters adored him. But his father, Walter Sr., condemned him, ostracized him and eventually turned everyone against him. My dad finally ran away to rebel against this bastard, and that was my dad's first heartbreak. That was the first notch in his spirit." Afeni grabs a smoke and looks me in the eye. "I'm glad you're here. I don't think about this stuff enough."

"It's *important* stuff."

"Yes, it's important to understand where your stuff comes from. As much as I hated my father, I can see now that he got beat up, too. Walter Sr. disowned him."

"That was his first notch. I assume there were others."

"Well, this is the way I see it now. Lord knows it was never something I talked about with him. I had as little contact with my father as possible. But anyway, after he left home, he wanted to serve in the navy. This was during World War Two, and he would have been proud to serve, but the navy rejected him because he had flat feet. As I look at him, I think this was his second notch. A huge blow. When he married my mom, I think he was *trying* to do the right thing. He saw my mom as a good person, a great girl, and by marrying her he'd have some place to do the right thing. But, as time went on, every time he looked at my mom he felt like a failure. He saw in her what he could never be, even though in reality she was satisfied with who he was; *he* was not. His father and the navy sealed my dad's coffin forever. He never recovered from those rejections."

"Damaged goods," I say.

"Damaged goods, and I understand that. I'm still glad we left him. We wouldn't have had a chance in hell had we stayed."

Time goes by and the night air cools the clean chicken bones piled on my plate. The unexpected visions of Afeni's father and grandfather drift slowly back to the haunts of her quiet memory. I feel like I know the short desperate man, Walter Sr. Muscular, tough, and angry. Determined to get his kids off the farm though he hasn't a chance for himself.

It's time for me to go. I hug Afeni one last time, or so it seems when I hug her, because like I said, she hugs that way. I drive back down I-20 to my father's house feeling full in my tummy and in my heart. Happy to have the daddy I have.

TWO

Up the Road

*"There were too many people full of hate and bitterness
crowded into a dirty, stinky, uncared-for,
closet-size section of a great city."*
—CLAUDE BROWN

I never know if I reflect the New York gray or if it reflects me. It is gray today, misty, and I am blue from all the gray. Afeni sits in the corner of the corner where she always likes to be. She is quiet and tired. She sucks on her Newport till it's all gone and drifts away in the smoke. Afeni and I can be quiet together. Even though it has been a year since I've seen her, we just pick up from our last visit in Stone Mountain. And today we are in my New York apartment being quiet together.

But this is no ordinary day. I'm packing up twenty years of my New York life in labeled boxes and Hefty garbage bags Afeni is here to sit with me while I pore over the last two decades of my gypsy life: Old Alvin Ailey playbills, signed cast photos, love letters, fan mail, my first 8x10.

Afeni and I have talked over the past year, but I haven't seen her face. Looking at her now, without the tall Georgian pines and sweet grass surrounding her, she looks more like she did when I first met her in the halls of 100 Centre Street. She's a little sad—contemplative.

So, we sit across the room from each other. I look out the window at a swatch of blue on the ashen street. A flattened Tampax box remains on the sidewalk after someone had ravaged the plastic garbage bags in search of recyclables.

"I hate when people go through my garbage," I say. "I hate seeing my shit all over the damn street. Last night, I gave that man five dollars so he *wouldn't* go through my garbage. I told him nothin' was in there. I even watched him walk away. I thought we had a deal. He must have come back in the wee hours and ripped open my bags. Or maybe someone else did . . . I'm just over New York! New York used to be my refuge. I came here for peace, energy, for some realness. But now it's just depressing."

I want to make a joke, but I can't think of one. I also want Afeni to think about something else, something other than what is making her eyes glisten in the dim lamplight. I want to bring her joy or fun, but I can't. I'm pissed. I'm pissed because I can't make her laugh right now. I'm pissed because my Tampax box is flattened on the sidewalk in front of my apartment for all the world to see. "I use the same tampons my mother gave me twenty-five years ago," I tell Afeni. "I like some things the same way they were first made. Even though they make a million different kinds now. A million kinds of everything: shampoo, toothpaste, soap . . . But some things are just fine the way they've always been. Johnson's Baby Powder . . . Vaseline . . . Q-Tips . . ."

"Tussy," Afeni interjects.

"Oh, my God, Tussy! My girlfriend used Tussy in the seventh grade. That was the first time I ever saw *cream* deodorant."

"That's right. Works just fine," Afeni adds.

"Man, Tussy . . . Jergen's! Jergen's Lotion." I remember. Afeni nods as she remembers, too. "My babysitter's daughter, Valerie, used Jergen's Lotion. In a glass bottle. She was a teenager. I loved that smell. . . . How about Bergamont? Thick, blue, rub-in-your-scalp Bergamont."

"Dax. Dixie Peach," Afeni offers.

"My granddaddy. Layin' dem waves down with some Dixie Peach!" Finally, we laugh, Afeni and me, as the scent of my grandmother comes to me.

"Cashmere Bouquet. My nana. My nana always smelled so good . . . soft. Pond's Cold Cream. Dove soap."

"We didn't have all those fancy creams growing up," Afeni says. "I'd just slap some grease on my legs, rub it in real good, and be on my way."

"Hair grease?" I assume.

"No, baby. Lard. *Grease.* Fat from the can on the stove. Kept me from getting ashy," Afeni starts a new Newport. "But that shit was thick, and by the time I got to school, walked in the dust, played in the dirt, my legs got all dark and sticky from the grease and the mud. Those kids laughed at my legs all streaked with black stripes. They called me Sambo and Tar Baby and, well, you know."

"Yeah, I know," I say. "A girl called Belinda Wilkey was damn near tortured at my middle school. She was long, bony, and dark. They ripped her apart every day. One day they threw her books on the ground, stomped on them, and then snatched the hairpiece right off her head. They called her 'baldy' and 'wildebeest.' I wanted to kick their asses so bad, but I was too little, and they were waiting for me, too. So I said nothing, although I wanted to be a hero. I wonder where Belinda is now and did she ever get over that abuse," I say in memory of my own school days.

"She got over it," Afeni says. "Or she's working through it. Just like all of us. We all are works in progress."

"Maybe she moved away. Maybe she came to New York like I did. The land of opportunity."

"Well, if she did, God bless her," Afeni sighs.

"When did you come here?" I ask.

"I was eleven. Sixth grade. But it wasn't exactly *here.*" Afeni surveys my tree-lined street from her perch across from the window. "No, it wasn't no Upper West Side brownstone. It was the South Bronx. Lots of concrete. Not quite what me and Glo had in mind."

"What did you have in mind?"

"You have to understand the whole milk-and-honey concept we had of going *up north*. Well, we called it 'up the road.' When my mom went 'up the road' she stayed with her cousin Wilhelmina in the Bronx. She got a job, then she sent for us. We didn't know the job in a factory making lampshades didn't pay shit. We didn't know our so-called house was a one-room apartment for all three of us. She tried to warn us that *up the road* wasn't quite what we were led to believe it was, but how could we imagine something we had never seen? I wanted some trees, some dirt, some rain, some sky. All I got was gray and soot. I was a tomboy with nowhere to run."

"I got here the summer of seventy-nine," I say. "Hot, stank-ass summer. I got off the train at Penn Station and took a subway to Forty-second Street. Oh, my God! Urine. Vomit. Steamed, porky hot dogs. Syrupy sodas. Dog doo. Underarms. Dirty feet. Morning breath. I almost threw up a few times on the subway going to dance class. All those strange people on top of me, next to me, and around me all the time. I learned how to cocoon myself on the train, though, make myself invisible. I learned to space out just enough to leave reality of the subway car and still be aware enough to watch my wallet."

"You learned how to disengage," Afeni says.

"I had a New York face and it worked—still does. I was determined no one would mess with me and, worst of all, no one would know I wasn't from there. Pure survival."

"It was the first year of integration at my junior high school. I walked through this park to get to school across the way," Afeni continues.

"You walked alone?" I ask her. "In New York?"

"Yeah. Well, my sister went to the high school. So, yes, I walked alone. You know, this is 1958, Jasmine. Kids walked to school." Afeni shrugs.

"Is that when kids picked on you with the Sambo, Tar Baby stuff, in the park?" I envision skinny Afeni up against a pack of preteen wolves.

"Byron Cohen said I looked like something from out of space." Afeni says his name like she'd know him today if he bumped into her on the street.

"What did you do?" I wonder.

"I kicked his ass," Afeni exclaims, surprised I had to ask.

"You could fight?" I ask, thinking of how much easier my life would have been if I had just kicked Velveeta Brooks's ass in the fourth grade instead of her kicking mine.

"Oh, yes," Afeni says. "All I wanted to do was fight—fight back. By the time I was in the ninth grade, I was pretty bad. I was giving my mama hell. I thought fighting was the way to compensate for my inadequacies. Before I learned how to fight, boys were always messin' with me. See, I was new. Dark-skinned. Short hair. And no titties! What was cute about that? And what is the only thing little boys think about at that age? Shit . . . being cute and titties. I saw myself in a different light. Boys made me feel ugly and weak. So, I'd go right to the source and beat the boys' ass. I had to have something else to offer besides being cute, other tools. I had a mind. I had a sharp tongue. And I could fight! I could fight right through my fear. If a pack of motherfuckers attacked me, I'd pick the biggest and the strongest motherfucker and fight for my life. That's why I always fought *boys* right off the bat, because if I could kick a boy's ass, you know I could whip a girl's ass. In fact, I didn't fight a girl till eighth grade. She was very large and very bad. And I was very scared and very small and alone. But I whipped her ass 'cause I was scared. Wasn't nobody in that cold, hard city but me and my mama and my sister. I thought I had to be totally prepared to stand up for my mother, my sister and myself."

"Like the man of the household," I said.

"That's right," Afeni said. "No uncles, no big brother, no cousins, no daddy. Just us in the Bronx. Country, naïve, and wide open. I had to stand up for us, and that's what I did. I got respect in the streets."

"I wish I had done that," I reflect ruefully.

"No you don't. Look at me. My anger destroyed me. You don't wish that. . . ." Afeni shakes her head.

"Afeni," I said. "Half the sixth grade wanted to beat me up. I was nine. They were eleven, twelve, and thirteen. They waited for me on a corner. They came to my house. My teacher, Ms. Lewis, had to drive me and my sister home from school because *she* was so scared. It's important to be able to protect yourself. Especially if you're always picked on for whatever reason and you're small. Please, tell me, how did you kick that girl's butt, Afeni? Biting? Scratching? Let me relive this moment with you and pretend it was me!"

"No scratching. It was a New York City school so we had to line up in the morning and at lunchtime. Downstairs in the gym with huge concrete beams and I slammed that bitch's head up against that beam. I lost it." Afeni palms this invisible head in her hand and bashes into an imaginary beam. "But what I really got in trouble for was kicking the assistant principal. She tried to intervene. But I didn't know who that lady was. She could have been one of the girls' crew for all I knew. That girl was big, and she had her clique. I knew if I went down, I was going to be stomped. I wasn't having that. After all, I am my father's daughter," Afeni explains.

"He was a fighter too?" I dust my grandmother's old crystal candy dish and wrap it carefully in newspaper.

"He was a fighting man, yes. He was a small man but unafraid, and he was stubborn and arrogant. That's what Tupac and I got from my dad—the rebellion and the need to fight back and be recognized for being different. We got that from my dad. Out of my mother, Glo and me, I was most like him; but that didn't mean nothing to me. In fact, it was an insult. Being the favorite of someone you have no respect for is not a compliment. From my point of view, he was always gone. I was angry with him, more angry than any of the other two women in the house were. I resented him."

"Did he scare you?"

" Me? I wasn't scared of him for me; I was scared for my very sad mother. When I used to come home from school, first and second grade, I would look under the bed to make sure he hadn't killed my mother and stuffed her body under there. I can see myself right now doing it. That was a real possibility to me, very real. When it was all clear under the bed, I would be relieved, and go on with my day. Well, see, that's what happens in a kid's mind when you have someone doing things secretly and it's not talked about openly. My mother was hiding everything. She was a good Pentecostal, highly religious woman. She tried to hide from her children that that bastard was hitting her. She couldn't hide it though, and I just grew to hate him more. 'Cause I'm seeing my mother who wouldn't hurt a thing, not even a fly. . . .

"So, yes, I was my dad's favorite, but it meant nothing to me. I was probably his favorite because I wasn't exactly respectful to him. I was a little fresh to him."

"It's hard to hate your parents," I say. "It's hard to live with that kind of hatred, because they are a part of you. So, in turn, hating them is hating yourself."

"I know. All that hating hurts. As a girl child, I just hurt. Everything around me seemed hurtful. And, like I said, we had no protection. I never felt safe. Now, I see that I got a lot from my mother. I have learned to appreciate her strengths, her quiet dignity. For most of my life I have been angry. I thought my mama was weak and my daddy was a dog. That anger fed me for many years." Afeni stands and walks to the built-in shelves on the other side of the room. She eyes a clear acrylic box I haven't packed yet. The box protects a pair of shiny pink toe-shoes. An honor I won years ago for teaching dance to kids. "In fact, years after we left my dad when I was on bail for my own trial, the Panther 21 trial, news came to me and Glo that the woman my dad had been staying with for the last ten or fifteen years stabbed him every which way but loose and he was dying. My dad's sister, Sharon, who me and Glo always loved, called and asked if my sister, who was a mother and a wife herself, could come and stay with him. My aunt Sharon couldn't take care of him, and Glo had just had another baby. So, I said, 'Not to worry. I will take care of Mr. Williams.' And that's just what I called him the whole time. I took care of him, too—'Mr. Williams.' 'Mr. Williams, you hungry? You need to go to the bathroom, Mr. Williams? Good night, Mr. Williams. . . . Mr. Williams, see you tomorrow, Mr. Williams.' I'm a mean bitch. . . . But he understood."

Afeni can be a bitch. I've seen her lash out at others, even though she's never lashed out at me. I try to imagine how far she could go with her own father, with her own son, or with her own daughter. I respect her anger, but I wonder how a man deals with it, or if a man ever did deal with it.

I need some music: Terence Trent D'Arby, first album. Afeni slides to the floor with her ashtray and her water glass.

"I paid dearly for being a bitch," she tells me. "I confused anger with strength and ran everybody off. At least that's what Pac used to tell me."

Afeni imitates Tupac: "'My mother is being so manly.' He used to tell people that shit and I dealt with that until the very end. I still deal with it after all this time. All I wanted was protection. That's all every woman wants. To feel secure. To be able to go through life knowing that a man in the street ain't gonna beat you up. Having a man to watch my back if I needed that. And all my life I have had to be the man. Then what happens is I get in trouble for being the man. That's the catch-22."

She is bitter, now, misunderstood and lonely, and I see why she doesn't like to go *back there. Back* to the Panthers. *Back* to past relationships. *Back* to old friends. *Back* to her husbands . . . I try to change the subject.

"Let's order Chinese." I grab a menu and the telephone.

Afeni shrugs. She's not a big food person. She eats because she has to. I wonder how good food can taste with all she smokes, anyway.

I do love some things about New York. One is take-out delivery. I'm going to try not to miss too much about New York. I know every move I make in this apartment is my last. I move out in five days. I have to pack it all up, and part of my heart is broken. I love the wood, the bay window, the hand-painted tile on the backsplash over the stove. The Alvin Ailey posters of past City Center concerts. The grand Steinway with chipped ivory keys that came with the apartment. "I'll take the piano" I had told the past owner. Even though I can't play very well, I knew that it belonged in this big room. I had the painters stain the wood trim of the mantel and bay windows to match the warm maple of the piano. The piano was at home in this apartment as was everyone else who ever visited me. This apartment embraced people.

It embraced Afeni and her family for sure. It amazed me that so many of them could fit so easily into this one room. Afeni's kids Sekyiwa and Tupac, and Glo's kids, Jamala and Katari, the grandbabies Nzingha, Malik, Imani . . . There are so many of them, but I could tell they could all live in one room without stepping on each other's toes. Like a Tokyo sidewalk at rush hour, so many people in one little space, but never in each other's way.

While I place the order, Afeni seems to have regained her peace. I wonder if she'll miss my apartment, too.

Scallion Dumplings, Special Fried Rice, and General Tso's Shrimp are on the way. I know Afeni and I are in for the night. A long night, probably talking until we fall asleep. I crack a window and light a black opium stick.

"I'm sorry, sweetness," Afeni says, "these cigarettes bothering you?"

"No, not really, I just like this incense." A house should never smell 'housey' to me. If it's not the scent of fried bacon and brewed coffee in the morning, baked chicken and yams at night, it should smell of black opium, red clover, sage, or Gucci #3. I lightly spray my Gucci cologne on a few lit bulbs. They sizzle and the scented steam rises through the air.

"Where did you learn that little trick?" Afeni is amused.

"My girlfriend, Gina. She probably doesn't even remember doing it herself. We shared a dressing room when I was doing *Beehive* at the Village Gate. She used to spray the hot bulbs around her mirror to get rid of that dank, musty smell of the Gate's basement. *Sssssss* . . . out came the steam of Jovan Musk. So, every time I squirt my lightbulbs at my house, I think of Gina, just for a second. It is so funny to me. Of all the things we've done together, of all the memories we have—Broadway shows, jokes, lovers, parties, and heartaches—spritzing my lightbulbs is the one consistent thing that always reminds me of her. . . . That is Gina's legacy." I laugh.

"It's a little thing but a big thing." Afeni smiles.

"Yes, it's a visit. Memories are visits." I spritz. "There. Gina just said 'Hi.'" The room is quiet. The scent diffuses, and we close our eyes to Terence Trent D'Arby. We listen for a minute.

"Oh, this boy can sing," Afeni swoons.

"Have you heard him sing 'I Was Born by the River?'"

"Sam Cooke's?" Afeni asks.

"Afeni," I warn her, "he wears it out. Let me see if I can find it," I look through my CDs.

Afeni gets excited when she's introduced to new things. She's a great person to introduce your passions to, and I can imagine Tupac bringing her songs and Sekyiwa bringing her babies and how happy they all must have been. She is a great receiver of art and love.

"Afeni, you have the soul of an artist," I say to her. "How did that happen? How did that live in you when you had no exposure to art? I'm not saying your family didn't have it inside, but everyone worked so hard. How did it come out if it was in there to be expressed? How did you become so expressive? And Tupac?"

"I don't know. I found out recently that my great-grandmother sang gospel from door-to-door. She spread the Word through song. As for me, I could always talk. My problem was knowing when to shut up. Articulating my feelings was never a problem. But I don't believe artists are cultivated like corn or cotton. Artists are messengers from God. They get here on earth and express themselves because of Him. I don't know where that stuff comes from. It seems to come out of nothing sometimes."

"Like the rose that grew from concrete," I say, quoting Tupac.

"Like the rose that grew from concrete." Afeni nods, affirming the reference. "The key is, and this is where we come in as parents, to guide the talent. Like for me, in my case, I never knew what to do with my thoughts and my mind, my mouth and my anger—I didn't have a place for it."

"Like your mother getting an education and not knowing what to do with it."

"Yeah, but I read everything. Reading works for me.

Reading gave me dreams. Reading gave me weapons. Like 'Invictus.' 'Invictus' is a powerful poem for a child.

Out of the night that covers me
Black as the pit from pole to pole
I thank whatever gods may be
for my unconquerable soul."

Afeni recites with the strength and inflection of Maya Angelou. She isn't loud, but her intensity grows as the words of "Invictus" come back to her. She is empowered again as she was as a child.

"It matters not how straight the gate
How charged the punishments scroll
I am the master of my fate.
I am the captain of my soul.

"And Shakespeare," she says, "which I was totally fond of. I read everything he wrote, not as an assignment. . . ."

"Couldn't have been an assignment. . . . You were never in any school long enough to get an assignment."

We crack up. Afeni shakes her head. "I know that's right. In and out. In and out. I was a mess."

"But you loved *Hamlet*."

"Yeah, I loved *Hamlet, Macbeth* . . . I know all those parts. Puck in *A Midsummer Night's Dream*. I loved Puck." She sounds as if Puck were an old friend.

"That's funny. Tupac loved Shakespeare, too. I thought he got this affinity from the Baltimore School for the Arts, but he got it from *you*." I'm not so sure why that is odd to me. Maybe because Afeni's love of Shakespeare does not fit my preconceptions of her. The reading gangster.

I continue: "And you know Tupac. He was like 'You don't like Shakespeare!?' with disdain and shit."

Afeni is laughing. "Yes, I know, and arrogant."

"Arrogant and mad like I disappointed him or something. How dare I call myself an actress and not be into Shakespeare? I found myself defending my taste. I read Shakespeare, but I don't have a passion for him."

Afeni's still laughing. "I's sorry. I's sorry I don't like no Shakespeare, Mr. Pac." She starts to imitate me groveling for Tupac's approval.

I join in. "Look, look here. . . . I love Langston Hughes and Toni Morrison, James Baldwin and August Wilson. . . . Please, don't think I's stupid. . . . I was like, boy, give me a break. . . . Everybody ain't got to like *Shakespeare*." We are both laughing now.

"Oh, he probably just wanted someone to talk to about it," Afeni defends her only son. "But see, you disappointed him." Afeni's laughter calms down.

"Yes. Don't disappoint Tupac," I say soberly.

We sit on that note for a while, reflecting the deep-seated disappointment Tupac held in his heart always. Both Afeni's children live life afloat a current of sadness. I wonder now if the sadness I see in Sekyiwa is grief, pain, or loneliness, just as I had wondered if Tupac's was longing, abandonment, or disappointment. Like Tupac, Sekyiwa can be sad in still and quiet moments. And like him, she loses the sadness in the flux and turmoil that surrounds her. Don't be quiet too long. . . . The sadness may come up again.

"Why were you in and out of school so much?" I figure it's time to get off Tupac and back to Afeni.

She speaks to me as if I should already know the answer to my question. "I quit or got kicked out. One school, I walked in the front door, heard Bobby Kennedy was killed, and walked on out the back door. I figured what the fuck. I had just had it. When I left PA, I was sort of asked to leave. I was given an ultimatum—

"PA? As in the New York School of Performing Arts? You were there!" I can't believe Afeni went to PA. Not because Afeni *couldn't* have gone or *shouldn't* have gone. It's just that PA was always a dream of mine after I saw the movie *Fame*.

"There were specialty programs that specific high schools offered and I was being evaluated as to which school I should apply to. My plan, what I wanted, was to apply to Hunter College High School . . . for reasons unbeknownst to me. My counselor at the time suggested Bronx High School of Science and the High School for the Performing Arts, why, I do not know. What I *do* know is that I wasn't allowed to even take the test for Hunter College High School. My IQ score was two points below requirement. I passed the test for Bronx Science, but I did not want to go there; too many rich white kids. I believed at the time that actors and performers were like free spirits. I thought I could relate to them better than some snooty white kids. But ultimately it was all the same shit. I was in over my head, way over my head."

"But PA is a public school. You have to audition to get in. It's not about money or tuition. Lots of brilliant, gifted people went to PA based on their own talent, not their money."

"A lot of the kids that went to PA were coming out of private schools. They came to school in limos, and I hated them with a passion. I'd get high off Thunderbird wine before school even started just to deal with my hatred of them. I'd get fucked up with my friends and then go to school and watch them rich kids' limos, pretty clothes, just showing off. This is what my mind was telling me back then, that those kids were showing off. But the worst part of the day was lunchtime. Lunch at Performing Arts was hell for me because they didn't have a cafeteria."

"No cafeteria? In a public school?" I wonder about the hot lunch number in the movie *Fame* when the kids start dancing on the tables in the cafeteria.

"No cafeteria. Kids would leave and go to Times Square or Nedick's or the Automat and buy their food. I didn't have money for lunch. My mother begged my bus fare off the neighbors just to get me down to the damn place. Lunch money and leotards and whatever else was out of the question. Are you kidding me? It was absurd to me, and

I was trapped. I couldn't tell my mother we needed even more money to go to this school. I wouldn't tell my teachers shit either. So, I'd just leave at lunchtime. Go to school, do my drama and dance classes and then leave at lunch. I missed all my academics."

"No one noticed you were gone?"

"They noticed, and they tried to get me to do right. This one lady, who used to teach Eartha Kitt when she was there, tried to get me to stay at PA. She told me how Eartha would work making dresses in the evening and go to school all day. She told me Eartha had a lot of problems, like I did. She said we were a lot alike . . . me and Eartha Kitt." Can you imagine—Afeni raises her brow, shakes her head, and chuckles.

I couldn't see Afeni at a sewing machine all night *or* in a cat suit. "Was Glynn Turman there at PA when you were?" I ask.

"Yeah," Afeni is casual, but smiles. "He was my boyfriend."

"Your boyfriend," I laugh out loud. "I know him!" I worked with Glynn on *A Different World*. He is a fine actor who worked with Sidney Poitier on Broadway in *A Raisin in the Sun* as a young boy, and he has been working ever since.

"I know you do." Afeni smiles.

"I like Glynn. Why didn't you stay with *him*?"

"Glynn's best friend went out with my best friend, Sandra. I loved Sandra dearly, but she was a little faster than me. So, she'd hang out with Glynn's friend, making out and what have you, and Glynn and I would be bullshittin', talkin', dreamin', hangin' out. I really liked Glynn. . . . I was in love with him."

Afeni and Glynn. Such a pretty couple in my mind; but, I know some shit must have gone down. "What happened to ya'll, all young and in love?" I wonder: "Break it to me gently."

"He liked big women," Afeni says as if she agrees with his bias. "Big women, like Ma Rainey." She smiles. "And he married Una. She went to PA, too. He should have married Una."

"Did ya'll break up or what?" I need more details.

"He slapped me," Afeni says.

"Glynn?" I'm appalled.

"For something I said," she adds pointedly. "I told you I had a mouth."

"I know, but still . . ."

"And I challenged him, talkin' about 'I bet you won't slap me again.' and guess what?" She looks at me.

"What?"

"He slapped me again," she says, and I gasp. "Slapped the fire out of me. I saw stars. And there's my lesson: Don't tell someone to slap you, because they may do it.

"I looked at the differences. Glynn lived in Greenwich Village. I didn't know no niggas that lived in the Village. And by the time he was at PA, he had already done TV, *Peyton Place* and *A Raisin in the Sun*. So, in my heart, I didn't feel I was on his level. After he hit me, shit, I was going to kill him. I came to school the next day ready to fight because that's what I knew to do. I was ready to throw down."

"Well, I'm glad you didn't," I say. "I like Glynn. He's a good man."

"I like him too," Afeni laughs. "He didn't beat me. He *slapped* me. I probably deserved it anyway. I was sixteen, and that's who I was. That's what I did . . . Fight."

"Damn," I say, laughing. "I can't imagine him slapping you. Well, maybe I can."

One day, months later, I ran into Glynn in L.A. at a café on Larchmont. He smiled when I mentioned Afeni's name to him. "You know, I only knew her as Alice, Alice Faye," he told me. "It was years before I found out that Tupac was even her son." His smile broadens as he remembers his friend. "That was my girl," he says. "She was so smart and so talented, but she was always talking about leaving Performing Arts, and that they'd kick her out. Eventually they did. But she could have stayed. She just felt like she didn't fit in."

I waited for Glynn to mention "the slap," but he never did. Mentioning it to him would break his perspective, and I was amused to hear how different Glynn and Afeni's recollections were of the same relationship. He never mentioned slapping her, just how he loved her fire. All Afeni remembered is that her fire got her slapped.

*　　*　　*

"I was too ashamed to really try in that school. I was too ashamed of myself," Afeni tells me. "I didn't think I belonged there, and I didn't know how I got there."

"Maybe God put you there . . . to give you a ticket out," I suggest.

Afeni shrugs her shoulders slightly, not completely dismissing my suggestion.

"Was your mother disappointed when you left Performing Arts?" I ask.

Afeni is quiet for a moment as her mother comes to her mind. I see the memory wash over her face. Regret comes into her voice for the first time. "I didn't do nothing *but* disappoint my mother, Jasmine. I broke her heart over and over again. . . . Rosa Belle. Rosa Belle Williams."

THREE

I Got a New Name

"I got a new name over in Zion.
It's mine. It's mine. I declare it's mine."
—NEGRO SPIRITUAL

For days I try to convince Afeni that her life is a movie. "Especially the New York 21 trial," I say. "That's definitely a movie. The drama behind the scenes. Your incarceration. Solitary confinement. The day they revoked your bail! Your closing arguments as you eloquently defend your life." I am excited. I pitch to Afeni as I have so many times to network execs. "You were a high school dropout, bright but unschooled. You came from the dirt roads of rural North Carolina and survived the streets of the lower Bronx. You fought through a violent, impoverished childhood only to rise to a high-ranking officer in the Black Panther Party." I come in for the kill—why this movie is important: "This is a sixties' story, a woman's story, a Black story, and an American story of survival."

Afeni looks at me. It is really quiet in the room since I stopped talking. Even though her face is calm, her fingers ferociously twist a small dreadlock on the side of her head.

"That was good." she says wryly, "You're a smart little bitch."

"Well, this is what I see."

"I don't know." Afeni ponders my pitch. "I'm better with books than with movies. Movies leave too much out. They're too manipulative. Movies dictate your feelings. They don't let you choose or decide where to go on your own. You have to give in to movies."

"And I know you hate giving in."

Afeni ignores my comment. "With books you can decide for yourself. You decide what to see and how to see it. Besides, I'm not up to convincing a bunch of mother-fuckers who don't even know me that this story is valid, interesting—or any of that shit. I don't want to meet nobody or to talk to nobody. You got to argue about how to tell the story and what the theme is and if there are any white male protagonists in the story so they can call De Niro. I know all this from Pac. It's bullshit. It's too many folks involved in making a movie. Too many cooks. Too many folks I have to trust or work with or whatever." Afeni's not having it.

"But it's all in the presentation. It's all about the screenplay," I say. "And our choice of directors is crucial. Let me help you envision this. We'll just do one scene, okay? Just take this ride with me for a minute. Now, since we are in New York, we'll do a scene from your life here. Maybe you can remember better now that you're back here. Okay, close your eyes." Afeni's eyes relax and close. I guess she realizes there's nothing to lose. "It's thirty years ago. Now, I'm going to tell you where we are and you just tell me whatever you can about this day. What do you smell? What do you hear? Who's with you?"

"In the scene," she muses.

"Yes, in the scene. . . . It is a Saturday, 1966, on 125th Street. Amber tones wash the streets and buildings. Yellow, tan, brown, and Black faces dot the sidewalks. They laugh. They frown. Some talk. Some hustle. Conga drummers pulse on the street corners. Bold headwraps of red, green, and gold bop in and out of markets. Processed dos slide down the street and glisten in the New York sun. Motown grooves from a passing cab window. Nina Simone wails from the eighth flight of a rusty fire escape. It is the day you find your new name . . . Afeni."

I wait and listen to the gentle hiss of the radiator in my living room. Small children shriek with glee on the sidewalk beneath my window. After a few minutes pass by, Afeni says, "*Four Women* was out that year. Me and Sandra loved that song."

Her eyes still closed, she starts to sway slowly, rhythmically, to a song in her head. She speaks softly at first. "*My*

skin is tan. My hair is fine. My hips invite you. My mouth like wine.
Whose little girl am I? Anyone who has money to buy. What do
they call me? My name is Sweet Thing." Now Afeni sings in a
deep, gritty tone. "*My skin is brown. My manner is tough. I'll*
kill the first mother I see. My life has been too rough. I'm awfully
bitter these days, because my parents were slaves. What do they call
me? They call me Peaches. They call me Peaches."

Afeni opens her eyes. They are distant and shiny.

"Sandra. She was my best friend. She was my best
friend, and she died. We were eighteen."

"What did she die of?" I ask.

"Neglect... She was pregnant. Didn't know it for a long
time, though. Earlier that year she was supposed to have
had a hysterectomy. But instead of doing what they said
they were gonna do, the doctor just took out one of her
tubes, and left everything else in there. And didn't even tell
her. That's how doctors treated poor folks... like animals.
Just do shit to your body and don't even tell you. She
thought she had everything else taken out. So, as soon as
she felt like screwing, she did. And got pregnant. But, like I
said, she didn't know for about five months, because as far
as she knew, her babymakin' days were over. So, me and
Sandra, we just kept doing our thing: hanging out, doing
dope, hittin' the clubs. And we tried heroin during this
time. This white guy, Henry, was taking care of Sandra, and
he gave it to us. He was white on the outside but he was
really Black on the inside. He was a street dude, and he was
good to Sandra. Didn't beat her or nothing. I liked him.

Anyway, horse made me sick, deathly ill, so I never did it again. But Sandra liked it, she liked snorting it. I found out later, after she died, she was skin-poppin' too. So, the baby's just growin' in there—"

"In the uterus she's not supposed to have," I say.

"And soon as she found out, she stopped druggin'. But something else was going on with her by then. One day after work—I was working at the post office—I stopped by to see her. She was looking good, too. Happy, you know? The last time I saw her she was just standing there in the doorway, waving good-bye to me. Later on that night, hours after I left, she collapsed in the bathroom. Brain hemorrhage, they said. Henry rushed her to the hospital, and she died right there on the table."

Afeni seems to eye the cold gurney and the heap of her friend lying dead upon it. "The miracle was the baby was born alive. But then the nurses came out, and they announced, real matter-of-factly, that they chose to let the baby die. No incubator. No resuscitation. Can you believe that? They just let that child die. . . . You know, being early and all, they could have helped that baby live, but they chose not to."

Afeni's eyes drip, but her face never changes. She talks right through the tears on her cheeks, as if they've always been there.

"That was the only friend I ever had, and I was very close to her. I saw her laid out on that gurney. Discarded. After she died, I just walked away. I couldn't even go home. I walked the streets for a day. I was fucked up bad. It was the first time in my life I'd ever felt someone's death. I can still see her alive with a pink housecoat on, with Henry. Happy. She was my best friend and I will miss her . . . forever."

Afeni's tears are big now. She wipes her face with the palm of her hand and goes to the kitchen for a paper towel.

"I am going to get to the day I change my name, though." She chuckles through the paper towel. "I haven't forgotten the 'scene' we're in."

"The pain of having someone die hurts so bad you feel like you can't breathe," I say.

Afeni nods and sits next to me on the couch.

"I consider myself lucky not to have anyone die on me while I was really young," I say. "My father lost his mother when he was eleven. It's horrible to experience that kind of pain that young."

"And it doesn't go away. And it doesn't get better. They said time would help." A sob breaks through her throat. "But it doesn't. It doesn't get better, and I miss my son," she pleads, "I miss my son."

Afeni leans on my shoulder and I rock her. Her body quivers as she catches her breath. Afeni's pain erupts out of nowhere, it seems. I used to think I was pushing buttons or, in some way, making her cry, but it is nothing I do. Afeni cries often, suddenly, completely. She feels gratitude, happiness, frustration, and loneliness intensely. She feels in bold primary color, not pastel. Anger is rage. Peace is joy. Sadness is sorrow. Grief is agony.

I hold Afeni until she comes back from the pain of missing Tupac. She is ready to go back to her story now, so I can learn about where she came from. In my mind I connect the dots of Afeni's childhood. I connect the eleven-year-old Alice Faye with the fifteen-year-old "Disciple Deb." I try to connect them with the fifty-year-old Afeni I know now. I picture her stalking Eighth Avenue in a pack of hard-ass girls. They drink Thunderbird out of paper sacks. They break antennas off of people's cars and then whip unsuspecting strangers with their new weapons. I picture Crotona Park and its public pool Afeni told me about. The water sparkles red under streetlights from the blood spill hours before. Razors. Knives. Ice picks and chains.

She rises from my shoulder and lights a cigarette. "I ever tell you about Ray? Ray was my boyfriend. I guess that's what you call it. Shit, he was thirty-three, and I was eighteen. We used to do things together. We'd go to all the events, discovering the new woman and new man we wanted to be. We would do LSD and sit on the fire escape listening to Jimi Hendrix and Sly and the Family Stone. And we would visualize, actually dream about being hit men. Contract killers. We wanted to be professional killers. . . . I think that was a common fantasy at that time. Black people were taking a lot of abuse. So, you would dream of yourself as somebody who could and would take care of some of the grievances. This is pre-Panthers."

I wonder how Ray the Hit Man is going to get us back to the day Afeni found her name. But I figure we can get back to the golden streets of Harlem some other time.

"What kind of events did ya'll go to?" I ask. "You and Ray. Where'd you go?"

"Be-ins, you know, with the hippies? Everybody'd get together and just 'be.' Political rallies in the park. We would go to those together. But after Sandra died, I dumped Ray. He was a womanizer and I couldn't deal with his petty shit anymore. After Sandra died like she did, Ray seemed trifling to me. I couldn't be bothered. So, I wandered. I would do stuff by myself, like go to bembes."

"What's a bembe?"

"A bembe is a drum ceremony to honor or call on an orisha," Afeni smiles. "See, I told you I would get back to your scene. There are your drummers."

"And my women draped in color and patterns from the motherland." I smile, too. "So, what is orisha, Swahili or something?"

"Yoruba. I studied the Yoruba culture and religion, and an orisha is like," she searches for a word.

"A god?" I ask.

"No, not a god. There is only one God. But orishas are like God's messengers. Each one is different and has its own personality, so to speak. Each one rules their own territory."

"Oh, like the gods in Greek mythology," I say.

"Yes, it's like that. My teacher, who introduced me to the Yoruba beliefs, said my orisha was Oya. She rules the wind, the tempests, and the Niger River."

"Well, that makes sense," I say to my tempestuous friend.

"There is more to it than that. It gets very involved, but that's the part I related to the most. I do believe that Oya is my deity. And I do believe in my name, which was also given to me at this time. Afeni, 'dear one' and 'lover of people.' This is what my teacher saw in me. That I was a lover of people. It's amazing with all the shit I was into, he saw me as a lover of people." Afeni is proud of this.

"But it fit, or you wouldn't have taken it on," I say.

"My mother never could pronounce my name, though. When she visited me in prison, she'd be the last one in line so no one behind her would hear her mispronounce my name." Afeni takes a deep drag. She sucks the smoke into her grim smile. "She mispronounced Panther, too."

"Ashamed?" I ask.

"No, not ashamed, just intimidated. My mother accepted what I was doing. She was proud that I had a voice, that I had the energy to fight and speak up for myself and poor, beat-down folk. She was proud of that because she never could have done that. She wished she had, though. I know that."

"But she couldn't say your name," I say.

"She was afraid to say any of it and bring it into being...." Afeni remembers. "I used to think she was weak, but now I know she was doin' the best with what she got. There are other ways to be strong. Other ways to fight your battles. My journey was completely different to my mother's. I can't even compare our lives, really. I grew very quickly. I learned a lot in a very short period of time. My lessons came to me through different people. . . ."

"Like your Yoruba teacher."

"Yes. But also people, just relationships I had. Like this dude Shaheem. He had been a Muslim under Elijah Muhammad [founder of the Nation of Islam and early mentor to Malcolm X]. I'd smoke some weed with Shaheem and just soak up this whole new philosophy of Black as beautiful, Black as strong. I mean, this philosophy was not completely new in historical terms. Garvey introduced this awakening in the twenties and thirties, but it was new to me, at eighteen. I was naïve and that shit Shaheem was saying about Black being the best color in the world and men should honor and protect their women, that shit right there blew me away. And this was the beginning of my awakening."

"A rebirth of sorts from Alice Faye to Afeni." My behind starts to tighten in my crouched position. I stretch my legs in front of me to get blood back into my glutes.

"Yes, but I'm not there yet. I knew even then that I was *about* to do something, and I waited for a sign to show me what that something was going to be. See, first I had to be open to receive any new information. Up until now I wasn't listening to anyone at home or at school. I've been in the streets doing whatever the fuck I wanted to. So, now this transformation has just made me ready to receive. The first thing I must do is be still. I must be still first, so I can listen. Listen and be still, and I already told you listening was hard for me."

"So when you stopped to listen what did you hear?" My legs fall asleep. I've been sitting on them so long the blood stopped flowing. I stretch them forward and lean over my thighs. I get so involved in Afeni's stories I forget. It's as if *I'm* roaming the streets of the South Bronx, as if *I'm* downing that nasty sweet burn of Thunderbird, as if I'm getting slapped by my high-school boyfriend.

"So, here's your scene, Miss Director." Now Afeni takes a turn at setting up the moment: "It's Saturday in Harlem and Bobby Seale's in town. Anybody who's anybody speaks on the corner of Seventh Avenue and 125th Street. Malcolm spoke at that corner. . . .

> *"If it must take violence to get the Black man his*
> *human rights in this country, I'm for violence*
> *exactly as you know the Irish, the Poles, or Jews*
> *would be if they were flagrantly discriminated against.*

"Marcus Garvey spoke there. . . .

> *"Men and women, what are you here for? To live unto*
> *yourself until your body manures the earth, or to live*
> *God's purpose to the fullest?*

> *"For two hundred and fifty years we have been a*
> *race of slaves. For fifty a race of parasites. Now we*

propose to end all that. No more fear, no more cringing,
no sycophantic begging and pleading...

"I'm telling you this is where you go to speak your mind and hear the word. So Bobby Seale's going to be there and I go just like everybody else goes. There are all kinds of folks there—mothers, hustlers, teachers, domestics, and kids, gangsters—all of us on that corner listening to Bobby Seale. He says the Panther Party is opening offices in New York, that they are coming and bringing change and order to our community, coming to heal the wounds of slavery and Jim Crow, coming to take arms against the aggression. They will not beat our ass anymore!

"Well, I have never heard nothing like that before. Then somebody on the platform next to Bobby Seale holds up a photograph. It is a picture of Huey Newton on the steps of the California state capitol, armed and standing tall. I see that picture of a Black man armed and looking the white man in the eye and saying: 'NO not laying down and getting stomped on over and over again.' When I see that! That is a powerful image for me." Afeni shakes her head at the magnitude of that day. Then she continues:

"And then Bobby Seale says the Ten Point Program of the Black Panther Party. Nothing sounds like Bobby Seale when he says the Ten Point Program of the party. He says, 'Number one: We want freedom. We want power to determine the destiny of our Black and oppressed communities. Number two: We want full employment for our people.

Number three: We want an end to the robbery by the capitalists of our Black and oppressed communities. Number four: We want decent housing, fit for the shelter of human beings. Number five: We want education that teaches our true history and our role in the present day society. Number six: We want completely free health care for all Black and oppressed people. Number seven: We want an immediate end to police brutality. Number eight: We want an immediate end to all wars of aggression—"

"That's a big one," I interject.

"They are all big ones," Afeni acknowledges. "'Number nine: Trials by juries of our peers; and ten, people's community control. . . .' It's longer than that, but you get the picture. Anyway, Bobby Seale . . . Bobby Seale saying that right there with passion, with intelligence. The way he said those ten points made me want that more than anything. So there I was wrapped in my Africanness. For the first time, loving myself and loving, now that there was something I could do with my life. There was now something I could do with all this aggression, and all this fear. Because up until this point, I wasn't shit."

I hate when Afeni puts herself down so completely, so unforgivingly. "Afeni, you were pissed," I say. "You were angry. You were a kid."

"Sweetness, let me tell you something. All the shit I was doing to people—against humanity. Robbing people. Beating people. That wasn't shit. Before I joined the party, I was fucked up. I would slap a motherfucker in a minute. I cussed my mama out, disrespected her, left her cryin' on the kitchen floor. Would you be proud of that shit? I left home and lived with any brother off the street that would pay my way. That's where I was! I'd cut somebody just for the hell of it and never look back. I told you, I liked to fight. I told you I had a mouth."

Afeni does not like to be denied, even on her own behalf.

"So, the Panther Party for me, at that time, clarified my situation," she says. "They took my rage and channeled it against them [she points outside], instead of us [she holds her heart]. They educated my mind and gave me direction. With that direction came hope, and I loved them for giving me that. Because I never had hope in my life. I never dreamed of a better place or hoped for a better world for my mama, and my sister, and me. I just never did. They took me and looked at me and said: 'Afeni, you are strong so use your strength to help the weak. You are smart, so use your mind to teach the ignorant.' And that's what I did. Sekou, my section leader in the Bronx. Lumumba, the section leader of Harlem. Kathleen Cleaver, Eldridge's wife and the only visual female force of the party. They were brilliant to me. I wanted what they had."

Afeni makes her point and closes her case, but I am not finished making mine: "I'm just saying that you had all of that in you before you met the Panthers. You discount that. Your own brilliance. Your own courage."

"No," she says, "No, I don't. My grandmama always told

me I was smart and would be a great teacher one day."

"But did you accept that? All I'm saying is when you dog yourself like that . . .when you discount all the stuff God gave you, and your mama gave you, and your grandmama gave you . . . you are doing a disservice to God. And you would not tell some seventeen- or eighteen-year-old girl at the Tupac Amaru Shakur Center for Performing Arts that she was 'fucked up.' You wouldn't do it. You would not tell some gangbanger off the street that he wasn't shit! So don't do it to yourself." There, I'm through.

Afeni looks at me, a little surprised. Basically, because I'm not scared of her and I think she's used to scaring people off.

"You owe me, like, five hundred dollars 'cause that's some shit you would have learned in therapy," I tell her.

"I guess at what point do you take responsibility for your actions?" she asks.

"I guess that is the question," I say. I don't know the answer.

"Well, let's go back to when I joined the party. That is when I felt most empowered. I believed in them." Afeni suggests.

"Believed in what?" I ask.

"The principles. The plan. I started the breakfast program to feed children on their way to school. I joined because I could use my mouth for speeches to raise money for the program. I joined 'cause I was fearless. I was a gangster, and I could do whatever was necessary to keep the party alive. I joined for free clinics. I joined for all that because it would have helped my mama if we had had that kind of help from our community. Those programs would have helped my mother with her two girls tremendously. And those programs would have helped my mother in a way that would have saved her dignity. I joined because the Panthers answered the needs of the people in my community. I believed in those programs, and I still believe in participating in your community, especially in schools. I believe in restoring your community, from the external structures of that community to the actual families. I believe it is the responsibility of every individual in a community to take back our schools, take back our minds, take back our bodies, and nurture our children. That is our job, then and now. That's where I am."

Afeni is quiet.

"And where does this philosophy come from, Afeni? Your mother? Your grandmother? Your father? Where does this sense of responsibility come from? Your teacher? Your great-grandmother?" I make her remember.

"I have always been dutiful—duty-minded, duty-bound. I am a big fighter for making sure a little girl takes care of herself to the extent she can. I was that little girl. And I fully understood there was a bunch I couldn't do. But what I could do, I would do based on what I knew to be true. James Cleveland says it best: 'You know when you know what you know what you know.' I think God always knows and gives you the ability to know. We don't all come here with the same assets, but we all have the ability to know. It is instinct. For me, it is not scientific, this ability we have. I know what I know what I know. I don't give a fuck what you say. I already know what's gonna happen, because God knows. That's what keeps me alive. That is what has helped me. And Jasmine, you don't want your daughter to lose her ability to know. She can not lose her instinct, because there lies her survival."

"Absolutely. When all is said and done, it is this truth, this knowledge within me that you're talking about that has always guided me. It is when I can not hear that voice that I have been lost and conflicted."

"*Shogun*," Afeni says. "Have you read *Shogun?*"

"No. I remember it was a miniseries with Richard Chamberlain. My daddy watched it."

Afeni shakes her head. I know she wishes I would read more instead of watching TV. "That book for me teaches the purist form of martial arts and how it relates to women. Duty and honor. Accepting your duty and finding honor in doing it."

"Like my grandmother." I remembered my nana, again. "She cared for my grandfather for ten years. Cleaned his bedding. Lifted his paralyzed leg and arm. Shaved him. Fed him. Wiped the drool from the corners of his mouth for fifteen years. My nana was only four-ten, a little thing, but strong, and she was adamant about caring for my grandfather."

"Of course, that's all the great wonderful people that we

want to grow up to be. They accept their duty and find honor in doing it."

"And you felt duty-bound to the Panthers?" I ask.

"I felt duty-bound to my people, my community, the mothers, and children of my community that were my mother and me and Glo."

"It was a great fight, Afeni, the war against oppression, the revolution, whatever you want to call it. And the soldiers were young, hopeful, angry, aggressive, intelligent, and vibrant. You were all so passionate and fearless."

Afeni seems to have left me for a minute. She seems to be remembering a time I cannot see. The main offices of Panther headquarters. A rally around the corner from her Harlem apartment. Dinner with Sekou and Lumumba, them telling me stories, war stories of white cops beating them up. Eventually, she comes back to me.

"It was a war that we lost," she says.

"Look at the forces against you, Afeni." I wonder if she's forgotten. "The COINTELPRO, CIA, J. Edgar Hoover, for God's sake. What about the spies? What about the double agents? What about the bogus charges? The constant court hearings and incarceration. What about the letter to Huey?"

"The war," Afeni shakes her head, "which we lost."

"What do you mean, you lost it?" I'm upset. "You were sabotaged. You were infiltrated, spied on. They said, 'Don't help your people. Fight amongst yourselves.' The Black Panthers imploded."

She says, "We dropped the ball."

"Afeni, the party was infiltrated, sabotaged. . . . What about COINTELPRO? The split between Eldridge and Huey? The phony letter to Eldridge? The arrests of Cochise? The bombings . . . the Omaha offices? What about the murders? The cold-blooded murders of Fred Hampton and Mark Clark in Chicago . . . ?"

"Baby, I know all this," Afeni interjects. "I know the mess."

"You said yourself there were spies in the party in your own Harlem offices. You told Lumumba, even before you all got arrested, that you smelled a setup."

"Jasmine, what I am saying now, what I know now to be true is this. We dropped the ball. Personally, if I, just speaking for me, had kept focused on what we were supposed to be doing . . ."

Afeni stops herself. She methodically snuffs out her cigarette, as if she's never done it before. She's thinking. She wants me to understand.

"There was a period in the development of the party," she says, "when, in answer to the unjust attack, we reacted—"

"Emotionally," I conclude.

"That's right. We lost it. We dropped the ball. We didn't know what we were dealing with. We were in over our heads. And, worst of all, we were not listening. We were not listening to old people. We had removed any semblance of spirituality from our movement. So, when the danger came, what did we have?"

I listen, fascinated by the tone of Afeni's admissions. I have never heard her speak so clearly about what happened to her once beloved Panthers. She is without resentment.

"Ultimately," she directs, "we are each responsible in a time of stress and trauma to hold that ground. Each person must be able to hold the ground on which they are standing. If the ground is not solid, you can't stand on it. Not having a spiritual base, not acknowledging the greatness of God, not saying we can't do this without God, we had no solid ground. Instead, we turned against God, and how you gonna win like that? You have to have a moral imperative to win. For example, that's the thing that Israel has lost which, ultimately, if they don't get that back, they cannot win. You can't do that in this world and expect that God is going to allow peace, harmony, and serenity to stay around you. We didn't understand that. We drew violence to ourselves. We drew bitterness to ourselves. That's my opinion."

Afeni snuffs out her last cigarette and balls up the paper from her Newport pack.

"We need cigarettes," she says.

FOUR

Love and Power

"Power is the highest object of respect . . .
We pity the impotent
and respect the powerful everywhere."
—FREDERICK DOUGLASS

With the shades drawn, the room seems smaller. Afeni is eating and is happily entertained. It feels safe for me to ask her now for the story of Lumumba Shakur, her first husband (but not the father of Tupac and Sekyiwa). Afeni met Lumumba and the Black Panthers at the same time. Her marriage and her life as a revolutionary are one and the same. Lumumba was her mentor, her lover, and her comrade. I am anxious to see what kind of man he was so I can see what kind of man Afeni likes.

"Were you in love with Lumumba?" I asked.

"Lumumba was my king." Afeni is matter-of-fact and I can't tell if she's being facetious or not.

"His whole family . . . the men in his family, his brother, his father, all of those men were good. From them I learned what men do in a family. What fathers do, what your husband's brother does, what your husband does. They were providers. They were protectors. When I met Lumumba's family, my entire view of men and family was shaken up. I went from this dismal, dismissive attitude of men, from having no concept of a man's true role or job in a family structure, to this beautiful, strong definitive and rigid role of a man's position in a family.

"The Shakur family was not only strong, but they were independent thinkers."

"And you liked that," I say.

"Oh, please," Afeni says. "This was the first family I ever knew to change their name. Lumumba's father was not only Muslim, he was also a Marcus Garvey follower."

I see the connection. The descendants of Garvey became the militant torchbearers of the '60s. Lumumba's father was a Garveyite, so of course, the logical progression for him to follow from Garvey and his Universal Negro Improvement Association was to Elijah Muhammad and his Nation of Islam. Marcus Garvey and Elijah Muhammad, two dynamic forces empowering the Black man in America. Revolutionaries. Separatists. Champions of a Black revolution. Internationalists. Pan-Africans. I know that Malcolm X's father was a Garveyite as well. The Garveyites became Muslims, and the Muslims became Panthers. Now this Panther, Lumumba, meets Afeni, his perfect match.

"When his father accepted me as the wife of his son Lumumba, I became Lumumba's wife. This all happened very quickly. I met Lumumba, married Lumumba, and joined the party, all within months. I don't remember how he proposed to me because it was all so fast. I was very moralistic and I wouldn't sleep with him without a commitment. So we married quickly because he wanted to have sex."

Afeni leans back on the couch. She watches the rotation of the ceiling fan.

"Lumumba introduced me to hot bean pie. We would buy them on the corner of One Twenty-sixth and Lenox. Bring them home. Heat them in the oven. Slice them up and eat the whole thing. Delicious. Sweet. We'd eat the whole thing . . . Just happy. . . ." Afeni chuckles.

She stirs up my memories, too. "I love bean pie. My daddy would go to the Muslim market. Get some fish. Fry it up and we'd have fish and bean pie. Oh, man. It was so good." I gratefully remember my daddy. "I'd have fallen in love with a man that brought me warm bean pies, too."

Afeni smiles. "Well, I did. But, like I said, we are all about morals and standards at this place in our lives. Lumumba, being a moral man, wasn't going to have sex with me unless we were married. Because he was Muslim, he did not need the white man's acceptance of our union. What we needed to be married in the eyes of Allah and our brothers and sisters was to proclaim three times in front of a witness that it was done.

"So his brother was our witness, and he just proclaimed to this brother three times that I was his wife. That is the least requirement in the Koran to get married. I didn't say shit. He said it. 'This is my wife. This is my wife. This is my wife.' I didn't know nothing about the Koran when I married him. All I knew is what he told me. Once I read the Koran later, I could see what a perversion this whole ceremony was. After I was in jail and I read, and had time to really read the Koran, I found out that there were really rules to being Muslim and being married as a Muslim. Lumumba didn't exactly follow these rules. But, like I said, I found that out later. I was accepted as his wife by his father and by everyone else in his family. And I joined the Black Panther Party in September."

"Did you like being married to Lumumba?" I wonder.

"Lumumba and I had a lot in common. We were both fighters. We both had good minds and we both came from the street," Afeni explains to me. "The marriage was good because me and my husband were fighting together. We were partners, and that's what I loved and respected about Lumumba. In his eyes I was a partner. Lumumba listened to me when I spoke. Lumumba and Sekou were best friends. They were the first men I had met in my life that didn't abuse women. They really seemed to love women.

That was beautiful to me," Afeni says. "And because of their position in the party—"

"They were high up in the party?" I ask.

"Yeah, Lumumba was section leader for Harlem and Sekou ran the Bronx."

"That gave you some clout, huh? Being married to a section leader."

"Yeah." Afeni calls it like it is. "Didn't nobody fuck with me because I was somebody in the party. They'd have to answer to Lumumba."

"You were protected . . . finally," I say.

"Protected and respected," Afeni smiles. "Lumumba was a great organizer. That's why the party did so well in New York. Back then in the fifties when Lumumba was coming up, gangs were run like little armies. They were organized and disciplined like the military. Lumumba was always a warlord or in charge of something. Even when he was in prison, he organized revolts and spoke out against the racist systems of Attica, Comstock, or wherever he was. He became very involved in the rights of the Black inmates, and his consciousness began there in prison with the teachings of Malcolm X. He followed Malcolm until he died."

"Why was Lumumba in prison?" I wonder.

"Aggravated assault," Afeni answers. "He got one day to five years for beating up a white man on a city bus. The man hit Lumumba first, punched him in the face for sitting next to him on the bus."

"Was that against the law then?" I am confused about where this happened.

"No, this is in New York. No Jim Crow. Not *legal* Jim Crow. I believe . . ." Afeni searches for the right borough. "Queens, Jamaica, Queens, 1958 or '59. Anyway, needless to say, he got locked up. The judge told Lumumba he shouldn't have retaliated when that man punched him, and Lumumba said that he believed in self-defense. So, they locked him up for the whole five years."

"And he was a juvenile." I can't believe it.

"He was under eighteen," Afeni seems bored. This is all old news to her. "But they did beat his ass before they locked him up."

"The cops?"

"Right there in Jamaica Hospital in front of nurses doctors, everybody. . . . Beat the shit out him and his friend."

Afeni drags on her Newport and takes a sip of Evian. Smoke glides from her nostrils like dry ice. "Police were always beating motherfuckers up," Afeni says.

"Like Rodney King."

"Yes, but for less than what he did. You go in for questioning. You get beat up. A man would get clubbed in the street in front of his kids because a pig thought he may have looked like someone who could have been the someone who committed a crime the night before . . . *possibly.*"

At this moment, Afeni reminds me of my aunt Clarie, who used to smoke but quit ten years ago. What reminds me of my aunt, though, isn't the smoke. It's the gleam in

Afeni's eye as she gears up to tell me a good story. That look on Afeni's face reminds me of Aunt Clarie, because they both know I like hearing a good story. And by good, especially in my aunt's case, I mean there's some blood, some guts, and some gore in the tale.

Afeni looks just like Aunt Clarie did the day she so nonchalantly told me about a lady who lived in a big house I admired.

"Yeah, Mrs. Sanders lived there. A widow," Aunt Clarie told me. "She had been dead for days before anyone found her. And by the time someone did find her, her two Doberman pinschers had eaten her body up clear to the bone." That's a typical Aunt Clarie story. Now, I wonder what gore Afeni's story might hold.

She begins, " Look at Joan Bird, my codefendant. I told you what happened to her."

I look confused.

"They beat her," Afeni says. "They tortured her. They hung **her** out a window and threatened to drop her. And when **they** were through, they slammed her into that rat-infested Women's House of Detention. She never received medical attention after she was beaten. They just left her in her cell to rot . . .

"And that's why, because of shit like that, when I saw that picture of Huey Newton on the steps of the California state capitol with a shotgun, in front of police and government officials just standing there with his comrades exercising their right to bear arms . . . that was powerful for me.

That was the first time ever I had seen a Black man exert his strength, defend his right right in the white man's face, and not get beat down, killed or destroyed. You have to understand, this is May 1968. Malcolm is gone. Dr. King is gone. John F. Kennedy is gone. Bobby Kennedy is gone. We were sick of laying down and getting stomped."

"So your attraction to the party and to Lumumba was the power it held for you. The power of self-defense. The power of change. And with Lumumba, the power of leadership." I begin to get a picture of Afeni's men—or so I think.

"When I saw Lumumba that first time, it was a rally for the Panthers in the park. There he was looking like something pretty with gold bars on his black naval three-quarter-length coat. They were red, black, and green bars. Red for the blood of the people, black for the skin, green for—"

"Money," I interject. Afeni cracks up. "No, I know. The land." I laugh.

"Lumumba was clearly running shit at that rally. He was busy and people were coming up whispering in his ear. The whole visual thing . . . This Black man as a soldier, a military person, and a leader. He could take care of me." Afeni drifts a little. "And I spoke up for myself, and he liked that."

"I thought the Panther men were a bunch of chauvinists. Macho, you know, with the whole Muslim influence and women knowing their place," I say.

"Well, first of all, what it looks like now or what it turned into is not the original ideology of the Panthers.

Their belief was that women were *not* to be treated as sex objects. In fact, the party gave me a platform from which to fight sexism. I had leadership ability, and I made use of that. I didn't feel like I was being sexually discriminated against because I *used* the tools they gave me. I spoke up for what I believed in. I spoke up for myself."

"Other women in the party were more passive or subservient?"

"Look, the women that got used in the party set themselves up to be used. They played pussy games. They used their bodies to get next to the power. Just to be up around it."

"Like a Panther groupie," I say.

Afeni shifts in her chair, like she's going to tell me some dirt. "I flew to Oakland to talk to Huey Newton about East-West disagreements in the party. That night I was asleep in my bed, and I woke up to somebody dipping between my sheets. I said, 'Excuse me. What are you doing?' And Huey [Newton] explained to me that I should be honored to sleep with him because he is the king, the boss, the president, and mastermind of the Black Panthers. I said, 'Nigga, you better get that thing away from me before I tell Lumumba what's really going on.' And he did." Afeni laughs, "We actually became good friends. See, I didn't get abused in the party because I chose not to be," Afeni continues. "And the women in the party chose to stay away from me, too. Their Panther men would tell them things about me like 'Afeni's a freak' and 'Afeni's gay' or 'Afeni's weird.' Women didn't want that association. Especially being gay 'cause then you don't get any men. But this is something I learned later. All I knew then for certain is that women stayed clear of me. The only women that were close to me were the women that chose what I chose. Women who were gangsters in the streets or women who had power someplace else before they even came into the party. A lot of women came into the party to get a man. That was not my goal or primary reason. Mine was always a matter of resistance. Men were just a means to an end—a way to fight against the oppression of Black people. I saw Lumumba was in charge of shit and I went right there. Right to Lumumba."

"So, you're like Hillary Clinton. If you're going to love someone, love someone who can get you somewhere. Partner with someone who can open doors," I say.

"The key word being *partner*. I was his *partner*. We made agreements. We had discussions. Lumumba loved my fire and my candor. He loved debating with me."

"What did you debate about?" I notice her choice of the word debate instead of argue.

"My using firearms. My seeing other men if I so chose, which I didn't. But, we had equal freedom in doing so as long as we understood each other's side. The most important thing Lumumba taught me was not to overcompensate. You know, I needed for people to know I was bad and strong. I was quick to speak out and volunteer for shit. So I would beg to be sent out on missions. I got sent on one once and I caused complete havoc. I still don't know how I survived. I shot at a man in a tollbooth because I wanted to rob something to show I'm so big and bad. You see. Bullshit. Give me a gun and let me go." She is sickened by her own ego. "I walked up, put the gun to the tollbooth, and said 'Give me your money.' The man slammed the glass and said 'No!' Okay? Can you believe that? I shot anyway, at the glass. Because how dare he say no to me, right? The bullet ricocheted off the glass. I had powder burns on my neck. Barely made it down to the car. The car is moving. People are shouting out their houses at us. We are in the white people's neighborhood wreaking chaos. Just don't know how I made it. That's why I know God is good because I was stupid beyond belief." Afeni shakes her head in disgust.

"Blinded by arrogance," I say.

"No, just stupid. These are the things Sekou and Lumumba worked with me on: my anger, my arrogance, my intolerance. The irony is I was arrested later for shit that I did not do, and the whole time I was thinking it was for that tollbooth incident. Humph, they weren't even thinking about that shit. They were talking three hundred and twelve years. That's what I was facing. They were like, 'Yeah, we got something for real for your monkey ass.'" Afeni gives a sardonic chuckle.

"That's the consequence of being in front, in being so visible. Sure, you are a partner. You have a voice. You running shit. The breakfast program for all the hungry little kids. Collecting bail money for all the imprisoned comrades. Encouraging the parents to take back public schools. Being involved. Speaking. Striking. Challenging. Fighting. But then you go down with the big boys, and the rest of the folk scatter. They hide, run away, or go underground. And you and Joan are the only women arrested with the rest of the men." Afeni accepts her responsibility. Then an old anger arises.

She goes on. "Price you pay," Afeni states. "Consequence of your actions. Thing that affected me the most is that it wasn't a consequence of my actions. I didn't do what they said I did. That's what I'm talking about. I knew my militant agenda would one day end here in the hall of justice, but there was no justice in how it was going down. We were spied on, infiltrated, set up, and psychologically manipulated. I saw people I thought I knew change before my very eyes."

"They were scared," I said.

"Shit, that's no excuse. I'm a woman, and I didn't succumb to the pressure that broke some of those men. That's what taught me the difference between a real man and somebody that talked a bunch of shit."

Afeni bitterly recalls the abrupt change in her comrades. Her eyes focus on mine so that I understand.

"Outside I was involved in Panther operations. I was doing things. I wanted to be a soldier. I learned to dismantle weapons, and I fought to train the women in the party to make them qualified soldiers. Lumumba loved my mind, and my fervor. Lumumba stood by me on my issues. We talked. We were open. I knew what he was about and what he was doing. Shit was on the table. That's why I didn't have a problem with him or polygamy. The issue was if I wanted another man then I could have that. I chose not to. If I chose to fire a weapon, that was my choice and I did that. All I had to do was to make sure he understood my reasons, then I did what I had to do. I had to respect him for that."

"What do you mean polygamy?" I didn't hear anything else Afeni said after that word. What is she talking about? Polygamy?

"Lumumba was Muslim and married under Islamic law. He had a wife and twins when I moved in," Afeni explains. "I was his second wife."

"You all lived together? In the same apartment? And that was cool?" I'm confounded. "You were OK with that? The other wife was OK with that?"

"Not at first. No, she didn't like it at first, but once she realized I didn't want what she had, I was no threat to her. She calmed down after a while. Besides, I didn't care. I don't think I cared about being an only woman. I never would give that much of my time to any one man anyway. It was a welcomed thing to me."

I am stunned.

"I thought his wife Sayeeda accepted it, or rather I chose not to see how miserable she really was. Because the reality was that she had not accepted that I came into her home with her husband and acted like I belonged there. I thought I posed no threat to Sayeeda because I didn't want her kids or her position. So I thought this whole thing should have been cool with her, but it was not."

"So . . . hold up." I feel so out of it. "Did you all sleep together in a big king-size bed?"

"No," Afeni answers calmly, like Colin Powell in a press conference. "He'd sleep with me sometimes. He'd sleep with her. She took care of the kids and the house. Stuff I was not interested in anyway. I was never very domestic. And me and Lumumba did our thing with the party. I didn't have no conflict. But it was killing Sayeeda inside.

"Lumumba and I were married in September 1968. By November, Lumumba and Sekou got busted in Connecticut on bogus robbery charges or some old nonsense. And there we were—me, Dharuba, and Cet—left in charge of the Harlem and Bronx sections for the Panther Party. I mean, look at that time, Jasmine. I had been in the party for six months, married for three months, and now I was in a position of leadership? I didn't feel ready. I didn't feel competent, but they told me I had to do it. I had to step up. There wasn't anyone else to do it.

"I was a section leader and I did my job. I took great pride in visiting my husband while he was incarcerated and being able to tell him that all he started, before his arrest, continued. We helped the PTA open twenty-eight public schools that the white teachers' union tried to keep closed. In Harlem, we organized the community and got a Black principal in a Black school. Because all the party's sections—Bronx, Harlem, Brooklyn and Queens—were assigned welfare centers. We were able to educate recipients about their rights and help them to receive their benefits. We also helped educate recipients and get them jobs. The community called on us, and we answered. I'm proud to know I was a part of that.

"You know, at this time when Sekou and Lumumba were set up, I did not believe I had the mind, the intelligence, and the wherewithal of Huey [Newton] or Kathleen [Cleaver]. I felt like a pebble next to them. But I went to those community meetings. I talked to those families, and up until March or really April second, we were really working smoothly as an organization with the people to gain control of our hospitals." As an aside, Afeni fills me in. "Lincoln Hospital and Harlem Hospital were known as 'butcher shops.' Black folk went there to die."

"Like Sandra," I remember.

"Like Sandra."

"So, at nineteen years old, you rose to the occasion, Afeni. You met the challenges of the Panther Party." I'm very impressed.

"Well, I didn't have a choice."

"You couldn't have done all that if you didn't have the ability to do it."

She hesitates, then looks at me and smiles. "God gave me a brilliant mind. I'm just now able to accept that. Back then, I always felt I was operating on a wing and a prayer."

Afeni lays her plastic fork down. She has had enough

fried rice and enough remembering for one night. She rubs her eyes and face as if to wash out her final vision. She's thin. She has long delicate fingers, like a pianist or a flutist. It is hard to envision the bulk of a metal gun in her hands, artist's hands. Tupac held a gun many times and his hands were just like hers. He definitely had his mother's hands, her body frame and her smooth chocolate skin. He was his mother's child in many ways. He lives in her.

"Good night, Fe. I'll clean up. Let me get you a blanket." I pick up the little Chinese food buckets.

"No, girl. We'll do it in the morning." It is a weak protest.

"I got it. It's easy. I am not leaving containers of food out in New York City. Roaches I can deal with, but if a mouse comes up in here, I'll have a heart attack."

Afeni is half asleep on the couch by the time I bring her a blanket. I go to my room and curl up in the one corner of my bed that I have not laid a box on or dumped the contents of a drawer on. It's cool. I have enough room to sleep. I think for a little while about Lumumba, Afeni, his other wife, and two little kids in this Harlem apartment. A commune. They lived like a commune. Everybody helped each other.

In the drawer of my nightstand lies my treasured copy of *Look for Me in the Whirlwind: The Collective Autobiography of the NY21*. After searching for months in used bookstores and the African-American Studies sections of every Barnes & Noble, I finally located this precious copy over the Internet. I didn't want to read it until I had finished talking to

Afeni about her arrest and incarceration. But I open it tonight because I can't sleep.

Oddly enough, Afeni recounts this period in her life almost verbatim in her interviews in *Whirlwind* thirty years ago. Afeni circa 1971 is refreshingly the same woman I know now. Her son was very much like her in temperament and in passion. They both have a surreal mixture of arrogance and self-disdain. Both were caught between fighting for more and not being sure they deserved it.

I turn the dried-out, yellow pages of the little paperback carefully, because they tear. Lumumba proves to be as interesting as I thought he would. He is sharp, articulate, convinced, committed . . . intriguing. I think Morris Chestnut, Denzel . . . Jeffrey Wright.

His chronology helps to give me a context for Afeni's life. Knowing Lumumba helps me know Afeni as a young woman. I begin to understand how much she loved and believed in the Black Panthers. Her admiration for these two men, Sekou and Lumumba, gave her a faith in men that she had never developed as a child. Above all, I begin to understand the devastation Afeni experienced at the split of her relationship with Lumumba and the demise of the Black Panther Party. He was released from prison in December 1964. He married Sayeeda, his first wife, in November 1966. They had twins, a boy and a girl, in February '67.

I read a few more pages about Lumumba before I drift to sleep. This is what Lumumba says of Afeni: *In the fall of*

1968 I got married again. My second wife, Afeni Shakur, possesses some qualities that I never saw in a woman. Her political consciousness combined with pure candidness, her directness and lots of fire. Afeni was in tune with my opinions in depth on political, military and matrimonial issues. Afeni never hesitated to give me constructive criticism on some of my actions. This I consider an asset to any revolutionary. Polygamy was no problem in my home because revolutionary principles and Islamic law govern my home.

If everything was in such perfect order, if Lumumba respected Afeni so much, where did that love go? If they were so perfect a revolutionary couple, what caused their demise? Was their relationship directly linked to the existence of the party so that when the party split so did they?

I wonder about Afeni and Lumumba. I hope she can tell me in more detail what happened to her. It seems to me that the life she had known for two years was dramatically destroyed. I flip to the end of the *Whirlwind* book only to find hidden in the back between the glossary and the publisher's notes a letter Afeni wrote to the children in her life while she was imprisoned. Afeni is twenty-four years old when she writes this letter on March 20, 1971, three months before her first child, Tupac, is born.

A Letter to Jamala, Lil Afeni,
and the unborn baby within my womb.

First let me tell you that this book was not my idea at all (as a matter of fact I was hardly cooperative). But I suppose that one day you're going to wonder about all this mess that's going on now and I just had to make sure you understood a few things.

I've learned a lot in two years about being a woman and it's for that reason that I want to talk to you. Joan and I, and all the brothers in jail, are caught up in this funny situation where everyone seems to be attacking everyone else and we're sort of in the middle looking dumb. I've seen a lot of people I knew and loved die in the past year or so and it's really been a struggle to remain unbitter.

February 8th when Joan and I came back to jail I was full of distrust, disappointment and disillusionment. But now the edges are rounded off a bit and I think I can understand why some things happened. I don't like most of it but I do understand. I've discovered what I should have known a long time ago—that change has to begin within ourselves —whether there is a revolution today or tomorrow—we still must face the problems of purging ourselves of the larceny that we have all inherited. I hope we do not pass it on to you because you are our only hope.

You must weigh our action and decide for yourselves what was good and what was bad. It is obvious that somewhere we failed but I know it will not—it cannot end here. There is too much evilness left. I cannot get rid of my dream of peace and harmony. It is for that dream that most of us *have fought—some bravely, some as cowards, some as heroes, and some as plain old crooks. Forgive us our mistakes because mostly they were mistakes which were made out of blind ignorance (sometimes arrogance). Judge us with empathy for we were (are) idealists and sometimes we're young and foolish.*

I do not regret any of it—for it taught me to be something that some people will never learn—for the first time in my life I feel like a woman—beaten, battered and scarred maybe, but isn't that what wisdom is truly made of. Help me to continue to learn—only this time with a bit more grace for I am a poor example for anyone to follow because I have deviated from the revolutionary principles which I know to be correct. I wish you love.

—Afeni Shakur

FIVE

Absconded

"I walked down the street didn't have on no hat
asking everybody I meet where's my man at?"
—Ma Rainey

I am not trying to hide the book, but when Afeni spots it on my bed atop the dune of blankets and sheets, I cringe. I feel weird, like I am spying on her. She has never mentioned the *Collective Autobiography* to me before, so I have assumed she doesn't want me to read it. Afeni always tells me about books, articles, art shows—anything she thinks I would love and/or learn from. So, this is odd. Why hasn't she mentioned *Look for Me in the Whirlwind?*

She flips through the small, old paperback book with interest but not particular care. "I wasn't very cooperative with this right here," she holds up the book, "and this right here, in the back of the book—'Letter to My Unborn'—was the one concession. They had to print this letter if I was to participate."

"I read it last night. But I almost missed it because they buried it behind that letter you all wrote to Judge Murtagh." I notice.

"You mean the letter *they* wrote. They wouldn't let me participate," Afeni corrects me.

"Your name is on it," I persist.

"My name is on it because it looked better to have all of our names at the end of the letter, but Sekou and Lumumba wrote it." Afeni flips through the book and then begins to read something to herself.

I switch the conversation to the parts of the book I find interesting. "I like Joan Bird's interviews." Joan Bird, Afeni's codefendant in the NY21, is the only other woman arrested with Afeni. She has big eyes, light caramel skin, and a long-shaped Afro. Her chin tilts down in her picture on the front page of *The New York Times,* and she peeks out from beneath her 'fro like she can't understand how she got in the newspaper in the first place. "She talks a lot about her life before the Panthers and what a shock the Women's Detention Center was for her senses."

"Yeah, Joan was a good girl. Catholic school. Hardworking parents. She was going to nursing school at night and worked with the Panthers on social programs and stuff during the day."

"So, how'd she get mixed up in the 21 arrest? I mean,

you were a prominent figure in the party. I can see them grabbing you. But why Joan?"

Afeni pieces it together for me. "Joan was arrested earlier in January of that year for attempted murder. The 21 arrest was in April. Right. She was arrested in January with Sekou and Kuwasi," Afeni thinks out loud. "Let me see what happened. Joan was with Sekou, and I know she got beat down by the police. She was in the car on Harlem River Drive, parked, when the police pulled up on the car. Kuwasi and Sekou ran and left Joan in the car alone. That's when the mounted police beat her and kicked her and treated her just like . . ." Afeni drifts away a little as she recalls the day she saw Joan after the beating. "When she came into court the next day, you could see the boot mark on her cape from where she got stomped. It was a plaid cape, and you could see the boot marks on the back of her when she stood up in court."

I am a little confused. "How did she get arrested for attempted murder by sitting in a parked car?" There is something missing.

"They said Joan, Sekou, and Kuwasi were parked there because they were going to shoot across the Harlem River into the precinct over there."

"Oh, there was a police station across the river. The police thought they were scoping the area to see how to shoot into the precinct?"

"That's it," Afeni confirms. "Now, dig this. When we all got arrested three months later in April, they added that attempted murder charge to our case, to the New York 21."

I take the book from Afeni and flip toward the last chapter, Part Eleven, where Joan Bird describes in detail the detention facility and its governing forces and routines. I read aloud to Afeni to see what she remembers.

"There is a big sign in the receiving area: 'You can write Legal Aid for a lawyer after you've been here for two weeks.'"

Afeni nods like she can still see that sign.

"The next act of degradation and humiliation comes as the women are told that we must take a shower. For those sisters who are addicts and are sick with chills and sweats, this is the perfect opportunity for them to die of pneumonia. After this shower we are given a dingy cloth robe to wrap around our bodies and a pair of rubber shower slippers to put on our feet. We are sent to the back of the receiving room to once again sit and wait. Then the prison doctor comes in to search our bodies, internally and externally. This part of the processing is a standard rule of the prison. Those who refuse to be 'finger searched' are then placed in a locked cell until they change their minds. The prison doctor goes along with the entire prison program in that he comes along when he wants to do searching, disregarding the bare fact that the women have been up for hours (up to ten hours) going through the prison authorities' 'procedures'

and are tired and hungry and want most of all to sleep. The women are called in to a dim and dirty office one by one and are told to lie down on an examining table with their legs spread wide apart, at which point the doctor jams his rubber-gloved index finger up the vaginal and rectal areas of the body. The authorities' attempted justification is that someone might be smuggling in drugs, weapons, chewing gum, cigarettes to take into the population. . . ."

"Now that's the part I refused." Afeni interrupts. "I took solitary over that shit."

"So you weren't examined either?" I ask.

Afeni looks over her reading glasses and lets me know with no doubt that she did not get that Pap smear. I continue to read.

"In the chaos of women sitting on benches and lying on the cold concrete floor—since there are never enough seats— each one is rushed into the doctor's office to face further maltreatment. Sisters are told to lie down on the examining table again and spread their legs wide apart so that this 'healer of the sick' can jam a surgical clamp up into the vagina, whether the person is a virgin or not, frequently causing hemorrhaging and severe damage to internal female organs. The reason given for this morbid procedure is that a Pap smear must be taken of every woman who enters the building."

* * *

KENNEDY

"No, I didn't go through that! No strip search. No filthy Pap smear. They just locked me down. And to tell the truth, I was exhausted. I walked in my cell, checked under the bed like I always did, and went to sleep. I slept through the rats, the isolation, the Spam, the fake white bread, and all of that."

"It's interesting how you and Joan are each affected by different things. Not that you *weren't* affected by the detention center, but Joan seems more sensitive, affected by her immediate situation, smells, food, despair . . . while you stayed focused on the *cause* and trying to make right what was wrong."

"She was sensitive like that, I told you, and they used her because of that. Because she was more trusting, more vulnerable."

Sure, she was sensitive like that, and she was the kind of Panther I probably would have been. A renegade social worker. Serpico in black leather. After reading all of the Panther autobiographies, I settle on Joan. She's the one I am most like—two working-parent home, home school, goals, future, socially conscious. I could have been used, too. Joan stayed in the car, and I probably would have, too. The detention center experience, being locked up like that, would have fucked me up, too, just like it did Joan. In the cold, dark, rat-infested corners of my cell, I would have missed my mommy.

"Afeni, you would have known to run like Sekou and Kuwasi. You know the street. You had a street sense. I would have stayed in that car, like Joan, because I would've been like: 'Hey, I'm not doin' nothing wrong. Why should I run?'"

"But both experiences are valuable. I ain't better than Joan!" she says, like a wise old sage. "Joan ain't better than me. We just saw things in different ways."

I love that Afeni embraces me for who I am. She's like the tough girls I always wanted to hang with in school but who would never let me in. I was smart and yellow and seemingly well off. They didn't realize that I knew them, like I know Afeni. They didn't know I recognized myself in them because they never gave me a chance. Afeni did not judge me when I met her. She didn't make assumptions about who she thought I was. I've always appreciated that in her. She didn't size me up and spit me out.

"You're right. I get pushed pretty hard before I fight back. You fight right away," I observe.

"And like I said before, that ain't always good," Afeni reminds me. "From the day, the moment, I was arrested from my sleeping bed on 117th Street, the fight was on. From April 2, 1969 until May 13, 1971. I fought for everything I believed in, against everyone I knew—not only the government, but my own Panther brethren. . . . And even Lumumba," she concludes bitterly.

"Ooooo, that's a good title," I say, thinking out loud. "The Five Battles of Afeni Shakur."

"For the movie?" Afeni says, a little less sarcastic this time than the last time I mentioned movie to her, and I am heartened by this sudden, if ever slight, interest in my idea.

"Yeah," I say cautiously, trying not to scare her off.

"I mean it may be more than five battles, but five sounds good . . . seven . . . seven sounds good, too."

"So, what are we doing? Just picking the ones you want to use? Because the real deal is probably like three hundred and forty-two." She laughs, "I was always fighting."

"The Three Hundred and Forty-two Battles of Afeni Shakur. Too long," I say.

"Well, I was in a constant state of battle."

"You're a soldier," I confirm. "Let's pick the big ones. The life-changing ones."

"Okay, Battle Number One." Afeni jumps right in as if she's been thinking of this shit all night, and maybe she was. "Obvious. The State vs. Afeni Shakur. Each of the 21 was charged with thirty counts of conspiracy. If we were found guilty, we faced a total of three hundred and fifty-six years in prison."

"Conspiracy to do what?" I ask.

"Conspiring to murder. Conspiring arson. Conspiring to bomb Abercrombie and Fitch, Alexander's, the Brooklyn Botanical Gardens, Bloomingdale's. . . ."

"Damn! Ya'll had that kind of manpower and ammunition? They thought you were Al Qaeda or something."

"Exactly. We were enemies of the state."

"What about all the community work the Panthers did? And where was the evidence of all this planning and organizing and acquisition of weaponry, et cetera?"

"Well, of course, this is to be revealed at the trial. Our defense attorneys . . . we always had a pool of lawyers hired from the beginning to defend us. In this pool was one female lawyer, Carol Leftcourt, Gerald Leftcourt's sister."

"Gerald Leftcourt was the main lawyer?"

"And this was his *sister.*" Afeni gives me the eye. "So, when they started divvying up the lawyers among the twenty-one of us, *they* took the male lawyers and gave Joan and me Carol Leftcourt, because we were women!"

"Who's divvying?"

"Lumumba. Sekou. Like they still in charge. Like they on the outside running shit. Like he still king declaring shit and making decrees." Afeni gets up abruptly to find her matches. She remains standing after her Newports's fired up because she's getting a little fired up too. "King." Afeni shakes her head. "Well, first off, let me say that this woman, this lawyer they gave me, Carol Leftcourt, had a tiny, squeaky voice. And I thought hell no, she can't represent me! Not sounding like that. The judge wouldn't be able to hear her *objection,* not with that voice. There was no meat to her voice, no resonance, no assurance."

"She didn't command respect," I add.

"There you go! Hey, I'm facing the same three hundred and fifty years everyone else is facing, and I am not going out like that. With this here, Carol Leftcourt, speaking for me? Shit." Afeni draws deep. "Battle Number Two: Lumumba vs. Afeni.' The fight to defend myself during trial."

"He didn't want you to?"

"Oh, please! Are you kidding? He said I was too emotional. He said I was not educated or qualified to defend myself and that I would fuck everything up."

"Weren't you afraid of that too?"

Afeni smiles. "I was young. I was arrogant. And I was brilliant in court. I wouldn't have been able to be brilliant in court. I wouldn't have been able to be brilliant if I thought I was going to get out of jail. It was because I thought this was the *last* time I could speak. The last time before they locked me up forever. I had to make a record there for later, because I would never be able to speak again. And I didn't know anything about being locked up either. I thought that when I went away to prison I would just have no contact with nobody. So, this was my last chance, and I had to make the best of it. I just thought I was writing my own obituary. . . ."

The words of Afeni's closing arguments ring loudly, sincerely, in Murray Kempton's *The Briar Patch*:

So, why are we here? Why are any of us here? I don't know. But I would appreciate it if you end this nightmare, because I'm tired of it and I can't justify it in my mind. There's no logical reason for us to have gone through the last two years as we have, to be threatened with imprisonment because somebody somewhere is watching and waiting to justify being a spy. So do what you have to do. But please don't forget what you saw and heard in this courtroom. . . Let history record you as a jury that would not kneel to the outrageous bidding of the state. Show us that we were not wrong in assuming that you would judge us fairly. And remember that that's all we're asking of you. All we ask of you is that you judge us fairly. Please judge us according to the way that you want to be judged.

"I just spoke from my heart." Afeni is suddenly solemn. She snuffs out her cigarette stub. "I saw this desperation in my son. Like he knew he was only here for a limited time. That's why it scared me so. I know that place Tupac was in. It's not a nice place to be. It's a place that will save you because you take yourself to the limit. To all the options of all the bad things that can happen. You take yourself there, and you accept them. I'm glad about that for myself because there are very few things that I am afraid of. In a crisis I'm afraid to be afraid. I don't allow fear to keep me from what I must do. I was afraid of going to jail forever, but I decided that if I couldn't keep that from happening I could at least go out in a certain way. 'If We Must Die,' by Claude McKay. You should read that."

Claude McKay, a writer I studied in school. Luckily I haven't packed all my poetry and plays yet. Afeni doesn't seem to mind the break. I don't remember the poem verbatim. I find one of my anthologies of Black poets and read it to myself. "If We Must Die" is stern and warlike. Very masculine. I see why the soldier in Afeni relates to McKay's call to self-defense. Written in 1919, it is a poem of empowerment.

If we must die let it not be like hogs
Hunted and pinned in an inglorious spot,
While round us bark the mad and hungry dogs,
Making their mock at our accursed lot.
If we must die, O let us nobly die,
So that our precious blood may not be shed
In vain; then even the monsters we defy
Shall be constrained to honor us though dead!

This call to die a noble death comes at a violent, vicious time in American history. A time when Black men were stolen, beaten, and hung for just being alive. The summer of 1919 was known as Red Summer. Race riots ignited throughout the urban cities just as the riots of the '60s explode in Afeni's time. The poem is a call to arms. A call for Black men to die with honor even when they cannot live with dignity.

O, kinsmen! We must meet the common foe!
Though far outnumbered let us show us brave,
And for their thousand blows deal one death-blow!
What though before us lies the open grave?
Like men we'll face the murderous, cowardly pack.
Pressed to the wall, dying but fighting back!

That is the line I remember from high school—*Pressed to the wall, dying, but fighting back!* My mind is on Tupac now and the last year of his life. He worked ferociously behind those prison walls writing screenplays, music, poems, raps. He cranked out hundreds of pushups a day on his knuckles instead of the palms of his hands. He complained of having "girl hands," so he beat them up until dark calloused knuckles adorned his fists.

"Let's get something to eat." Afeni rises and stretches her legs.

Coming out of my thoughts of soldiers, "I have to finish packing," I say halfhearted. "The movers come today."

"We'll get a sandwich. Bring it back," Afeni suggests. I realize *she* may need to get out of the apartment, and we're only on Battle Number Two. . . . There are many battles to go.

At the Chinese-Cuban restaurant on Broadway and 78th they don't sell sandwiches, but an order of arroz con pollo with black beans sounds better than ham and cheese on rye anyway. This is comfort food I know Afeni will eat.

"I want your plantains if you don't." I call Afeni's food like I'm calling my favorite seat in front of the TV before anyone else gets it.

"Well, I do," Afeni says. "So we best order extra."

We eat in the restaurant quietly. Afeni seems tired of talking, and I enjoy the peace while I watch people on the streets, especially when they are not watching me. The human interaction on a New York block is incredible. With the families, couples, teens, nannies, drunks, every social combination of a neighborhood is right here on one corner of one city block.

When we return to my apartment, I flop on the couch. I'm tired for no particular reason. I'd love to watch *Oprah* 'bout now and rest my mind, but Afeni's ready to move on. We trudge through another battle, Battle Number Two, her ordeal with Lumumba.

"Lumumba and I started fighting even before we got arrested," she explains. She seems weary of her marriage being referred to in loving terms, and wants to set the record straight. "Part of the propaganda of the party was to present me and Lumumba as a super Panther power couple like Kathleen and Eldridge Cleaver.

"But it wasn't really like that. I was pushing and pushing for women to have more rights in the party. I felt we were all soldiers, together. I pushed for weapons training classes for the women. My section always had weapons training courses. I would lead the Political Education classes to ensure that we were learning the same thing the men were learning. From dismantling weapons to using them. We were soldiers. Lumumba kept telling me women weren't qualified. 'Train them, and they will be!' I argued. And we fought about Yehwah because I knew he was a fucking cop from the very beginning and Lumumba wouldn't listen."

"Is that Ralph White . . . Yehwah?"

Afeni rolls her eyes and nods yes.

"How did you know *he* was infiltrating the party?" I ask.

"Because he was a hothead. He would come around the Panther office wearing his gun. Shooting at shit. I have a good sense of male character, and I knew that this man right here is not a stand-up person. He ain't gonna fight nothin' . . . He ain't gonna do nothin' . . . in life. He's a pig. He's too arrogant for a Panther. He roars up to the office on his bike. He just rubs me wrong. He says he comes from the streets—the Bronx, and I know the kind of people from there. And he ain't fitting in none of that. He just didn't act like a Panther." Afeni shrugs. "But Lumumba didn't listen, so—"

"So you ended up questioning him yourself at the trial."

"Yes, and what comes out in trial is that Yehwah had slept with Sayeeda and he was—"

"Sayeeda! Lumumba's wife?"

"And he was pumping her for information about Lumumba and me." Afeni takes a drag off her cigarette as I digest this new revelation about Sayeeda.

"I told you she didn't accept it," Afeni says. "We acted like she did, like it was OK what we were doing, but she didn't accept it. I came into this woman's home, this woman with babies, and acted like it was something right about what I was doing. And, well . . ."

"She gave away your secrets," I say.

"And I questioned Yehwah in that courtroom. Looked him right in the eye and asked him if he *knew* that I had done something wrong and unlawful, and he said 'No.' And that was that. So, whether she gave away my secrets or not, Yehwah still had no case against me."

"Wow! That's a trip," I say, recalling a passage in the *Whirlwind* book. "Lumumba talks about that relationship like it was cool."

"I know, girl, I know, but what I did destroyed that woman. Ate her alive slowly. She drank cough syrup all day to deal with that shit. Addicted to cough syrup . . . and me and Lumumba'd be pissed if we came home from whatever we had been doing in the streets and dinner wasn't ready. No, I owe Sayeeda nothing but my deepest apology for what I did to her."

"Even though she retaliated that way?" I ask.

"Yes. Absolutely," Afeni says. "I understand what she did, and I'm sorry for what *I* did. But let's get back to Battle Number Two. So, basically, Lumumba and I are fighting. He wants to run me in prison! He wants sex, and I refuse because to have sex in prison, under those conditions, is some slave shit to me. There is no freedom having sex in those terms. Two prisoners! Two incarcerated Negroes waiting for a chance to sneak behind Massa's back for a few minutes of fucking. That was a disgrace. I refused. Although I know people would have made it happen for us," Afeni says with disgust.

"Like how?" I wonder. How do you screw in a big visiting room or holding area? I thought there were always guards or other inmates around.

"Well, we were all in separate detention centers around the city. They made sure to separate us," Afeni recalls. Thirteen of the twenty-one were standing trial together. So to meet with our lawyers, before court, we would all be together in one room. Briefly, but just so they could say the codefendants had time together with their lawyers."

"So, Lumumba wanted you to do it there? In that room . . ."

Afeni shrugs.

"What? Everyone would just turn their heads or something?"

"Slave shit. On the plantation." She spits out the "T" in shit.

"So, how long did you abstain from sex?"

"Prison sex," Afeni corrects me. "Eleven months. It was eleven months before those women could raise my bail. Bail was set at a hundred thousand dollars. A hundred thousand dollars! We didn't have that money. That money had to be raised. I remember Glo and her husband, Tom, came down to the bail hearing. They had scraped together every dime they had from every neighbor they knew to get that hundred dollars. But the judge said one hundred *thousand* dollars, and he meant one hundred thousand, not ten percent of that. I had never heard of that many zeroes. I couldn't believe it. A hundred thousand dollars. In 1969!

"While I was in the Women's House of Detention I built relationships with white women who needed to touch the hem of your garment so that they could be made whole.

They would write me and visit me and ask me what they could do to help. Well, there were all these women inside who only needed fifty dollars to get out of jail. So, I asked these women to form a bail fund for women in jail who needed less than five hundred dollars for bail.

"I figured I might as well get them out since my bail was impossible to raise. Nobody had ever done anything for these women before. A lot of them were just prostitutes whose pimps were mad at them and wouldn't bail them out. But they didn't have fifty dollars. So they just stayed in jail." Afeni notes some of them had kids.

"So these women from the outside who wanted to help *you* ended up helping other inmates?" I ask.

"This was my first contact with a lot of white women," Afeni explains. "And these women tried to help. Of course, there were those white women who wanted to know if I knew a Black man interested in having a baby with them because they wanted to have a baby that's coffee-colored who they could name 'Coffee' . . . I wanted to crush a bitch for asking that shit."

"Stupid," I say.

"But I spent eleven months in jail until some of the *well-meaning* white women who helped collect the bail fund were able to raise *my* bail money. These women had been in the labor movement in the forties and fifties, and they got together with my family and the women from the church and put up sixty-six thousand dollars in cash, thirty-four thousand in church property. It was amazing." Afeni gets full from the love and support of these women. She sees now how rare that support can be in life. She is grateful all over again like it was March in 1970 right now.

"They had to go to court and sit on the stand and justify every single dime before the court. Then they allowed me to get bailed out, and I was the first one to get bail, out of the 21. Then it was my job to raise money to get the others out. Joan was next because she was a woman. Jamal, because he was young. Dharuba, because he was a good talker. And Cetewayo—" She stops abruptly.

"What?" I'm very involved by now in the story, and I want her to keep going.

"I'm starting to get pissed," Afeni says, and she reaches for her Evian. "This right here is bringing up some bad feelings for me."

I don't say anything for a while. If she wants to go on, she will. If she doesn't want to, she shouldn't have to. But damn, she is leaving me hanging.

I resume packing. I can't believe how many books I have. You'd think I was a genius. I even have duplicates from buying copies on both coasts. A heavy feeling sits on my chest as I realize my "bicoastal" days are over. Time to be a mother. A new life ahead.

Afeni walks to my bedroom window and stares out on the backyards of the other brownstones. She is sitting on the radiator cover. She opens the window, sets up her ashtray and lights up. "The 21 were going to kill Dharuba and Cet because they weren't doing their job on the outside. They weren't being loyal. They were egotistical maniacs. I was speaking everywhere while we were out on bail. I busted my ass to raise more money for the other 21; and those two didn't do squat. During this time, the party itself was ripping apart. Eldridge Cleaver was a major force in the party. People think Huey, but it was Eldridge. He may have been the most intelligent member of the party. He and his wife, Kathleen, were brilliant. Eldridge was very charismatic and strong, and people liked him. He was building an international base with the Panthers—Cuba and Algeria. In fact, Eldridge was in Algeria while I was out on bail."

"And Huey wasn't having that, I'm sure. Someone with all that power in his party." I imagine that clash of egos.

"So people started picking whose side they were on within the party—Eldridge or Huey. Then they started pressuring *me* to pick sides even though I was fighting for my life at the time, and I was five months pregnant! Askin' me that shit. They didn't ask me how I was doing or if I needed anything. It was always about the party and which side I was on.

"All the time I'm out on bail I'm working on my case, too. I'm reading and studying and building my mind. Fidel Castro's closing statement in his trial, 'History will absolve me,' gave me the tone of my defense. Which was that you admit to what you're going to admit to. You straight up say: This is what I'm responsible for, and I can stand on this, and the rest of this is irrational. That was the first time I had read anything that powerful, and it touched me. Because I was in that position of being accused of stuff I didn't even understand." Afeni is intense, gripped by memory.

"That's where my head was. Saving my life and saving my unborn child."

"So you were still going to court during all this."

"Oh, yes. We are in the middle of trial. We have the biggest FBI agent on the stand. And then on a Monday, it was February 3, 1971, when Joan and I got off the elevator. We could feel something was wrong. We walked into that courtroom, and our codefendants hadn't shown up. Our bail was revoked. It had been revoked before, but that was for being late and stuff like that, and they let you out. Now it's revoked because people have absconded. My codefendants, the men—Jamal, Dharuba, and Cet—gone. In the middle of trial! The jury sees this. Joan and I are now back in jail, and I'm pregnant. Yes, ma'am. We went straight to jail, and the next time I came home was a month and three days before my acquittal. The same women that bailed me out before bailed me out again. God bless them."

"The men just didn't show up? After all that money was raised?" I am stunned.

"Absconded." Afeni nails the words into the smoky, bedroom air. "Jumped bail. And they had the right to, you know. Every individual has to do their own time, so you can't tell somebody else not to jump if they want to. But we had an agreement, that if anybody didn't want to go in, they would tell the others. So, they jump bail, the men. And not only did they not tell me or Joan, they left the country under the pretext of supporting Eldridge in Algeria. Talkin' about they had to take care of some party business with all that was going on. Bullshit!" Afeni is spitting out words. "Punks!"

Then she abruptly announces, "Battle Number Two! Battle for the Baby." She sounds triumphant now.

"Uh-uh, Fay, we are on Three." I correct.

"Really? We almost up to Five?"

"Yeah, Look . . . Number One, you fought against being strip searched. Number Two, you fought to defend yourself. Number Three, you fought Lumumba about having sex while incarcerated. . . ."

"Oh, wow! We might have to do seven then, because I didn't count that strip-search thing. That didn't feel like much of a battle to me. And I forgot to tell you what Lumumba did when he found out I was pregnant."

"Oh no," I realize, "and it wasn't his baby!"

"It wasn't a battle, really, now that I look at it. He was just enraged. Here I was not having sex with him but partaking with other men. Which I told you, we had an agreement that we could do."

"Right. As long as the other person knew about it." I remember their trippy vows.

"Well, I had never acted on that before. I never went with some other man even though we had an open relationship."

"You really didn't have time to have an affair. You were married for five months before Lumumba got arrested.

Shit, three months after that you were in jail, too. Not a lot of time to get some booty on the side," I say.

"This was the first time I went outside the marriage. Then I got pregnant, which I didn't even think I could because up until now, let's see 1971, I'm twenty-four years old. I had never gotten pregnant, so I didn't think I could. I was really surprised to be pregnant. So, Lumumba called me a slut and said three times 'I divorce thee. I divorce thee. I divorce thee.'"

"And that was it? No screaming. No tears?"

"Well, after the trial was over, and he got out of jail, he asked me to please take him back. But I said I didn't think so."

"Damn," I say, "I marry thee. I marry thee. I marry thee. I divorce thee. I divorce thee. I divorce thee."

"That's it. But look, I have a lot to deal with at this point. Now, I'm in jail and pregnant and that Spam and water crap they called food ain't cuttin' it. But to get decent nourishment, I have to go to court. So, I go to court to get an egg and a glass of milk each day for the baby in my belly."

"Did you win?"

"I won. I had support from women during all that. Women have to find strength from other women, because that is what gets us through. The shit that the old lady told you and the women in the jail have told me when I was pregnant . . . that old lady told me to put Vaseline on my belly so I wouldn't get stretch marks. The old woman that talked to me when I was crying and heartbroken because the niggas had left me and they took my bail. It was the old women that took me off that eighth floor elevator, took my clothes off my body and washed them, put toothpaste on them so they were starched for the next day, and told me to go in there tomorrow and shame them."

"Battle Number Four."

The trees outside my bay window burst with color. It's a warm autumn day. A clean fresh breeze hits my face, and I smell detergent.

"I love when people do laundry. It deodorizes the streets, like a giant stick of Tide incense blowin' in the wind."

Afeni nods. She's reading the paper and only halfway listening to me, but I continue.

"I wish it was gloomy like yesterday and a little colder. With trash blowin' down the sidewalk and the odor of fresh dog doo wafting in the wind. It would be easier to leave New York if it was being ugly. Well, at least the movers are late." I look at the time. "That's one annoying Manhattan trait I will not miss."

Afeni looks up and over my neatly stacked and numbered boxes.

"It's up to sixty-five," I say regarding my last box count. Can you believe I have so much stuff?"

She shakes her head. "I can't believe it all fit in this apartment."

"What time does Ebony sing tonight?" I ask. Ebony Jo Ann is a gifted, robust nightclub diva with chocolate skin and a vibrant smile. She is also a longtime friend of Afeni's. "I wish I could go, but I'm tired and sore. I just want to soak in some Epsom salts, pop a few Advil, and go to bed. I'd love a *Law and Order* marathon tonight."

"I'm leaving around seven. I'm not staying too late because I have an early flight in the morning. I think it leaves around 8, 8:45 something like that." She swigs her Evian like it's a jug of moonshine, but she doesn't resume reading.

"Are you going to be all right?"

I smile at her for knowing how I can get. "I'm ready to say goodbye," I assure her. "I may cry a little but that mouse I found scurrying across the carpet last winter kind of helped seal the coffin. Let's say I have closure in leaving this apartment."

"And like I told you, there'll be others."

"Thank you for keepin' me company while I packed. It went by fast with you here."

Afeni rests the empty plastic bottle against the couch and picks up her paper again. "The next time I see you," she states with finality, "we're moving on from this subject right here. I got more to my life than my Panther years."

"I know, Afeni. I know. It is just that a lot happened to you in a concentrated period of time. From nineteen years old to twenty-four you had this accelerated life . . . just like Pac," I realize out loud.

There are comparisons I've conceded with Afeni and her son. The eleven months they each spent in prison. The rivalry between East Coast and West Coast rappers in Tupac's life and the rivalry between East Coast and West Coast Panthers in Afeni's. They both had sharp minds and quick tongues. They are both socially conscious and politically involved. Tupac is definitely Afeni's son. But this is the first time I realize how young they both were when they were thrust into America's revolutionary arena. 1968–1971 for Afeni and 1992–1995 for Tupac. They both lived fast and hard.

Suddenly it occurs to me, "Maybe it's not a movie, though. Maybe it's beyond the courtroom drama . . . " I suggest.

She looks at me like she can't believe I'm saying this. "I *know* it's not a movie. It's a *book!* Like I been saying it is. A book. And not another Panther book either, thank you." She gets up from her chair abruptly. She seems exasperated, bored even, with the Panther subculture.

I finally concede. "Okay, Afeni. Hold up. Let me get some paper." Afeni settles down in the corner of the couch, folds her legs, and pulls out a smoke. I am excited. I can't believe we are really going to do this. We are really going to tell her story.

"Help me clarify some shit first," I begin. "I need to make a timeline. I'm confused with the ins and outs of your detention and when the pretrial ended and the real trial began and all of that."

While I talk, I am trying to remember which box I have packed my office supplies in so I can locate a legal pad. "Do what you gotta do," she says offhandedly. "But you know I'm not that good with dates."

"You remember the *key* dates. We'll work around that." I find a blank notebook and I sit with Afeni on the couch. I use a couple of boxes to write on. "April 2, 1968," I say, fixing on a date. "You say they busted into your apartment and apartments all over the city and arrested twenty-one New York Panthers. Who is 'they'?"

"They," Afeni answers readily, "are members of the NYPD Bossy Unit. That was a special division of cops straight out of the police academy that were young enough and stupid enough to infiltrate Panther offices and operations. I say stupid because they had no savvy, no smarts about our situation and what the Panthers were trying to do. They treated us like thugs and enemies of the community. . . . Yelled Fire! Fire! In our apartment hallways. Slammed into our bedrooms, knocked our children to the side, pressed a pregnant woman to the floor belly down, jammed a gun into my stomach and a gun into my husband's face—and called *us* thugs."

"OK. You were arrested on April 2, 1969, and you were released on bail January 30, 1970. Your trial didn't begin until September 1970. I'm confused about that eleven months before you were bailed out and what was going on for a year and a half before the trial?"

"First of all, know that at this time, 1969, 1970, this

NY21 trial was the longest trial in the state's history. The pretrial hearings didn't begin until February second, ten months after we were arrested. Second, State Supreme Court Judge John Murtagh halted pretrial hearings for an indefinite period of time. This had never been done before, and after I think four weeks of this delay a letter was written to Judge Murtagh from the Panthers demanding a fair trial."

"The letter in the *Whirlwind* book?" I ask. "That condemns the justice system and confirms how futile it is to have a fair trial in America?"

"Yeah, that one." Afeni twists a small dreadlock on the back of her head.

"How long were you out on bail?"

"I got out on January 31, 1970. Trial began February. Dharuba and Cet absconded February eighth of the following year."

"Seventy-one" I'm writing. I'm going to have to make a timeline, I think.

"Seventy-one," she confirms. "I got pregnant while I was out on bail. I never thought that I wasn't going to spend the rest of my life in jail. I was never getting out and that's why I wanted to have this baby. Because I wanted to leave something here. I was going to jail for three hundred and twelve years. That's what I was facing. But my sister was out. If I thought I was getting out, I never would have had the baby. I probably would have gotten an abortion."

I think how hard this is for her to say knowing what a beautiful baby she did have and knowing now what a life she had with her son. But that was her truth then, and I know it was true because of the certainty in her voice. It had to be true. And maybe it isn't so hard for her to say as I think it is. She has lived this truth and worn this truth for many years. Maybe it's not that hard for her to say. It's just really hard for me to hear.

"There were a hundred and ninety-six felony counts," she continues. "There were twenty-one of us arrested and thirteen that went to trial together. When that Black man, who I later found out was a master of classical music—"

"What Black man?" I ask.

"The jury foreman. When he got up and said a hundred and fifty-six times for thirteen people: not guilty. He made it a ballet. That Black man stands up and makes it a ballet with two words: not guilty. He says it in every tone he can say it in. Ingram Fox. I'll never forget him. He was West Indian. My husband is the first one to be read. And by now the courtroom is shrieking. Because if Lumumba is off, then everybody is off. Lumumba is the hardest part of the case. If anyone is getting convicted it is him. So, when he isn't convicted, we already know. . . ." Afeni smiles and looks at me directly. "The jury was out for ninety minutes. When they sat down, they took one vote, and they miraculously voted the same: not guilty."

"This was all highly publicized in the New York press. I mean Murray Kempton followed the case closely, and followed you in particular." I get up because I remember an article I want to show Afeni. I hope I can find it.

"Murray Kempton was there every day in that court-room. God bless him. That's what his book *The Briar Patch* is about. The New York 21 trial."

"He followed you till he died," I call out from the bedroom. "I saved these articles. I was so impressed with his passion for you. Do you remember the *Newsday* article he wrote about Tupac after he was shot here in New York? During that whole abuse trial?"

She nods. Of course she remembers.

"But, Afeni, this is the one I wanted to read to you. Sometimes it's good to know what other people see when they see you. Sometimes I feel like you are just stuck on a rigid opinion about yourself, and I think it's enlightening to hear how Murray saw you." I begin reading aloud from Kempton's description of Afeni at the NY21 trial:

"This was entitled 'From a Sleek Panther, A Slick Thug.' I'm not going to read the whole thing," I assure her.

"She would emerge from there for each day of trial thereafter wearing the frock of a country girl in trouble. . . ."

"This is after they absconded," Afeni clarifies. "When me and Joan get locked up the second time."

"So you were pregnant?" Afeni nods and I resume reading.

"Suddenly there was even more life in her presence than there had been in the crimson pants and the saucy boots her jail keepers had put away.

"An afternoon arrived when her turn came to cross-examine Ralph White, the undercover policeman she had known only as Yehwah in the days when his lips were sworn to the Panthers and his duty was to gather evidence against them.

"Afeni Shakur stood up for their engagement with her shoulders staunch and her stomach helplessly swelling with Tupac and with the supreme beauty that is the vulnerable girl asking with her eyes, 'Why are you doing this to us, Yehwah?' And then she transformed this using male from her antagonist to the sharer of common memories. She has somehow managed the miracle of crossing the great void between the rebel and the counterrevolutionary; and they began talking about her perilous and his endangering past as intimately as if they were alone.

"Near the end Afeni Shakur gently asked Ralph White if he had ever seen her do a bad deed. He replied that he couldn't remember her doing much and that all he knew was what she said.

" 'I see,' Afeni Shakur said. That short word protracted its resonance in the air while Ralph White departed and she went back in the dock to sit dreaming with Tupac, the work done on this day when it became impossible to think that she and her baby and the whole odd lot of her codefendants had not been saved from jail. Their trial had lasted nine months, and they were acquitted in two hours."

Afeni is quiet throughout my reading. When she speaks,

she is reminiscent, subdued. "I remember that article. It was a strong piece, very insightful."

"Very much in your favor. It was a piece to remind you of what you are and what you are capable of."

"And before cocaine kicked my ass, I believed it. Yes, I believed I was this—what'd he say—Sleek Panther. I believed I did carry truth and integrity in my heart and in my words. I raised my children to believe it, but I faltered. And that is Tupac's story. His mother faltered, and that was devastating for him. I can't deny him *his* story. My addiction is part of *his* story, and my daughter's, too.

"I wanted to skip to the head of the class. I wanted to be up there without doing the work or learning the lessons, and God said: No. No. You got to learn. I can't blink my eyes and get there, fast and furiously. In fact, it's better not to go than to go that way. . . . No, Tupac was right to tell his story. At first, I felt raw, exposed, and betrayed. But that was his right, his story to tell. Tupac was right."

"And Murray Kempton was right, too. That's all I wanted to say."

"Sweetness, I understand what you're trying to say, and I appreciate it. But I can't afford it. My ego, my arrogance can't afford it. I have to deal with reality—truth. Not half-truths, not kinda truths—facts. And this right here [she pats Murray's article], is true, yes. But it is not completely true because it eliminates my arrogance."

"Are you substituting arrogance for confidence when you say that? Or arrogance for courage?"

"No, dear heart, I know the difference. I defended myself in the trial of my life to leave this earth with the records straight. I had not done the things I was accused of doing. I had not committed those crimes. I was right. I stood on that righteousness. That is strength. But what was arrogant was, for an example, going to court high. High on sunshine, this little orange pill that made me trip like LSD. I was going to court trippin'. Sometimes, before pregnancy, when I was in jail, people would give us cocaine through the lawyers. A lot of cocaine, and we would sniff it real quick. So I would do that. But then I'd be in court objecting—on sunshine. I didn't hallucinate, but my mind would trip. You can only do this if you are young and stupid. Arrogance. It was arrogance that gave me the right to waltz into Sayeeda's house with her man on my arm and say, 'I'm the second wife. Move over.' How dare I? What the fuck was all right about that? And *I* looked down on *her* because she was raising her kids and I was out on the streets being a 'soldier.' Me and Lumumba would come home from whatever we were doing in the street and dinner wasn't done. Sayeeda was drinking cough syrup all day. That's how she dealt with her pain." Afeni spews in self-disgust. "Damn! The children ain't got nothing to eat, but I'm a soldier woman. I was wrong, and there is no way I need a light shining on that like it was something gorgeous. I was a stupid bitch. I owe her the deepest apology."

Afeni is clear, real clear. And with that clarity comes

calm. Even though her stories are wrenching, chaotic, and wrought with violence, the peace she has made with that avenue of her life, the acceptance she has found in who she is and why God made her, rings louder than pain or remorse.

"So this is what I know. For me, for Afeni . . . I just have to stay in touch with reality. When my brother-in-law told me I wasn't really an addict, when he suggested that I *didn't* have a problem, I wanted to believe that so much I got the fuck outta there."

"Out of Tom and Glo's house?" I ask.

"I was smokin' cocaine in their bathroom! And he's trying to tell me I don't have a problem."

"But you were functioning," I say. "That's why they couldn't see your addiction. You were still Afeni to them. They couldn't see how it was bringing you down," I offer then I think again. "Or maybe they were in denial."

"But I am not that kind of person. I couldn't afford to hear even the *suggestion* that I was not an addict at the time. I was just getting clean. I had my own justifications for my drug use. After it all disintegrated, and I was alone with my memories and nowhere to go, after I watched them kill our men and lock up their brilliance, I made choices only an addict can make.

"My addiction was not just to substances but also to the people I continued to keep in my life. I stayed right there with those people. I never moved on. All the time these men were being killed viciously, being arrested, disappearing, and

I just stayed. I believed in my heart that this was it. These people were my life. I didn't know that I had a choice to get out of it. Not until after my recovery. I didn't know any better. Even when I was smoking crack at my worst, I would say, 'God, how am I gonna get out of this?' And He would say, 'Well, for you there is no way out. Where would you go?'

"I thought the reason I was getting high was to quiet the vision of all the people dying and all that violence and trauma. So, I would say stuff like, 'If you stood in my shoes for one second, your ass would be high too.' And I believed it."

SIX

One-Time Story

"He lifted his hand and I flinched.
And I hated myself for being so weak."
—GLORIA JEAN COX

I wake up at 2 A.M. This is nothing new, as I'm an insomniac. I don't want to turn on my TV because it will awaken Afeni. So I tiptoe to the cabinet looking for green tea, honey, and Jif creamy peanut butter. I glance toward the family room and I notice Afeni sitting upright on the couch. Her face is toward the bay window, and I cannot tell if she is asleep or not.

"I'm awake," she says without turning her head.

"What're you doing?"

"Thinking," she says.

I don't think that's good. I know how thinking too much can make you crazy. "Want some tea?" I ask.

She shrugs, and I fix her some anyway. I weave around my boxes to get to the couch without spilling a drop.

"How was Ebony?" I ask, knowing that I missed a fabulous show. Ebony's voice is rich and deep like the mahogany color of her skin. When she sings, you know she knows life—love and sorrow, and hard times and parties.

"Good. Wonderful. She just got me thinkin'."

"About what?" I wonder if Afeni wants to talk.

"Baltimore," she says and her voice goes down. It sounds like she's dreaming or talking in her sleep. "Everything changed in Baltimore. Everything." Afeni says with the longing of a hungry child. Afeni's "everything" spans thirteen years across the bridge of prison to freedom. Through the love of birthing her baby boy. Over the dunes of marrying her friend, Mutulu, who gave her a daughter. Afeni's "everything" includes her important work at Legal Services helping the disenfranchised and searching out the women and children abandoned by their Panther mates. In those years Afeni watches the men disappear underground, sail away to Africa, and get arrested. Afeni's "everything" encompasses the reentery of Afeni to society, the thriving in her environment, and the slippery slide back down as Mutulu Shakur is arrested. Legal Services lets her go and Afeni loses her apartment. Slip-sliding back down to the bottom of the barrel, Afeni sees Baltimore as a new promise, a chance to start over.

So, in 1984 with thirteen-year-old Tupac and seven-year-old Sekyiwa in tow, Afeni takes off to another urban jungle in hopes of saving her life.

"The first two years in Baltimore were good." Afeni sounds dreamy like I'm not even there. She twists her hair and stares out the window. A street lamp reflects a twinkle in the glaze of her eyes. "I didn't do drugs there. Baltimore was a heroin town, and my drug of choice was cocaine. So, I just smoked weed in Baltimore, and I was just a mom for the first two years. I just took care of the kids. Got them settled in school and all."

I picture Afeni packing Tupac and Sekyiwa's lunches and being calm just being a mother.

"After I lost my job at Legal Services, when they let me go, I was lost. I loved that job, too. Mutulu, Sekyiwa's father, had been helping all these Panthers. Panthers in Algeria, Panthers underground . . . And I think I lost my job because of my association with him. I had Sekyiwa by now, anyway. Sekyiwa and Tupac. I lost my apartment and moved in with Glo and Tommy. But really, they had enough on their hands already and Glo had the idea about Baltimore. Sharon, my father's sister . . . her daughter had an apartment in Baltimore and let us move in. And I saw that as a way to start over. I tried to turn my life around. I was just a mom. I went to school with Sekyiwa. Sat in on her class, went on field trips . . . I was a PTA mom."

Afeni is lost in this time of her life. Ebony's singing dug up memories, clearly.

"I was on welfare those first two years. My second year I requested to be put into a computer-training program. I went to computer school every day from eight to three P.M."

This is the first time Afeni speaks of Sekyiwa as a little girl, and I see the love in her eyes. While Afeni talks I also hear Set, Sekyiwa, all grown up, weaving her tale around her mother's. There is an unspoken honesty—sometimes easy, sometimes raw—that colors Afeni's stories.

As Afeni tells her story I hear Sekyiwa in my mind. I hear her song. It wails, moans, and murmurs through Afeni's voice. Sekyiwa's are dulcet tones in harmony with Afeni's rounded and grounded blues. I hear it like a duet between mother and child.

"I moved to Baltimore for a better life," Afeni begins.

I hear Sekyiwa's answer: *We lived in Baltimore for four years. The first two years were the happiest for me. We had weekends over my Aunt Sharon's. We had things to do. Nothing political. We had noodles, and it was fun. It was regular people's life.*

"I was on welfare the first two years, but we were happy."

She was isolated for the first time in her life. Separated from my Aunt Glo and her family. She was depressed, deeply depressed, I found out later. I didn't know how unhappy she was until later, but I was just a little kid.

"All my friends, my associates were gone, incarcerated, dead, underground. After Mutulu was arrested and jailed we just laid low in Baltimore."

I went to private school in fourth and fifth grade. Basically, an all-white school. I was one of three blacks there. They had a field trip to visit the FBI building, and I came home and told my mom I didn't think I should go. I didn't go to school the day of the field trip and sure enough when I went to school the next day, the kids were like: "Oh, we saw your dad! You look just like him." That was when he was one of America's Most Wanted. They saw his picture on the poster.

"Set, as a young person, was more peaceful than peace. One day her teacher called me up crying about Sekyiwa. She said my daughter was too good for this world. . . ."

She told my mother I wouldn't survive in this world. I was too sweet. And she cursed that teacher out.

"I cussed that bitch out. It was a cop-out. There's no such thing. What are you saying? That she's a sweetheart, but she can't be protected? That's what I responded to. . . . She ain't too good for shit. She lives in this world. She's a sweetie pie. She's gonna hurt. I knew what that teacher was saying. She was saying Sekyiwa wouldn't survive. And my response was that she would. I was like: Fuck you. She's my baby. I'll protect her."

I don't think she wanted to change who I was, but she wanted to give me strength, backbone, even if I didn't use it. I could use it if I needed it and eventually I did. When I needed it, I was able to dig down to the lessons my mother taught me. She told me pain is given. Suffering is optional.

"Sekyiwa's rage came later. Set was dangerous when enraged. She would take it across the line. She never knew what danger she was in. It's so complex. She was a banshee. Uncontrollable. She sought to hurt."

I remember her and Pac in the living room talking, and I would just listen. Lessons about my period even, or cleaning, inde-

pendence or whatever . . . I got it like that through her talking to Tupac. I guess I wasn't old enough. But, by the time I did go through puberty, she was unavailable. So, whatever I learned from her telling Tupac is what I had to go on. She explained stuff to him about a girl that he was seeing or having sex with and I picked up information about myself through conversations she had with him.

"What you have to give your child is their rage, and they have to get themselves through it. And you need to be there to help if you can. I was not there for Sekyiwa. I abandoned her at a time she needed a mother, as she was becoming a woman."

One time, Tupac was getting picked on at school about his clothes or not being flashy enough, and my mom was trying to teach him that he was more valuable and he wasn't into flash. She told him that he was more valuable and he was of good quality . . . that he didn't judge things by their covers, but by their value. Then she said, "if there was a crumpled up hundred-dollar bill and three shiny pennies, Set would pick up the shiny pennies and you [Tupac] would take the crumpled up bill, 'cause you [Pac] know true value." Even at eight, I knew that that was an insult, and it wasn't true to my personality. But that stuck with me.

"All I ever had was my brain. So, with my son, who was my first and only child for four years, with my son right at the beginning it was important to me that he and I communicate."

She always told us what was going on. She was up front about her situation. She hadn't had a boyfriend since I was three. And she said if she was going to bring someone around us it would be some-one who could help us. Someone we could grow from, and he wasn't.

"My cousin was a Muslim, and he introduces me to this guy from the mosque, and he was nice. We were cool, and the sex was real good. So, we kinda had a relationship."

He was the splinter that broke everything.

"I was working at night. I had a bank card. Money came up missing. I also discovered he was snorting heroin in my basement. I told him he had to leave because I got kids."

When she let him in, this was a real betrayal . . . like the drugs. Because she always told us she would never do that.

"I told him, 'Look, you're getting the fuck out of my house,' and I must have known I was getting older and couldn't do this crazy shit anymore. I went to the phone to call 911, and he slapped the phone out of the wall and punched me in my face five times in succession. Then he went out the back door. That started me not wanting to be at work. Everybody saw my eyes, and they knew. But I still went to work."

My mother was a proud Panther woman, the strongest. You don't get beat down like that.

"Tupac wanted to beat his ass, and I made him promise not be beat up the man. Tupac was sixteen at this time and never forgave me for not letting him protect me. Like I allowed that man to do that to me, but I didn't allow him to handle it. Sekyiwa was living in California by now. So at least she didn't have to see me with two black eyes."

Afeni has stopped talking, and I don't know how long it has been quiet. My mind spinning with the Shakur women's stories.

"I'm going to tell you something just once," Afeni says, still facing the window. Her eyes sparkle in the spill of the streetlamp. "Since we are writing a book and all . . . I can't rightfully leave this out. But I'm tellin' this story *one time*, then I don't want to talk about it again."

"Okay," I agree, my dread rising. I kind of just want to watch a bad movie or a good infomercial right now and try to go back to sleep. Somehow I know, after this tale is told, I'll be up for the rest of the night. I wait for Afeni to light up her Newport and finish her one-time story. What can be so bad, I wonder, with all Afeni's been through, what can still hurt her so much? Afeni lights up and walks around looking for her makeshift ashtray I threw out hours ago.

"Where's that Coke can?" she asks.

"Use this." I give her a real ashtray, bright red, from Atlantic City. "I don't know who gave me this, but I'm not packing it."

She sits Indian-style on the floor facing me. She sounds steady at first like she's retelling an old tale. "The last two years in Baltimore were not good. I had sent the kids to California, to Marin City, to stay with a friend named Asante, Cochise's wife. The plan was for Tupac to get his math credits so he could graduate on time. Baltimore School of the Arts had fucked up and not told us that he was delinquent in his math credits. So, we find out late that he can't graduate with his friends. Now, I understand that Tupac and Jada were great assets to their fund-raising efforts, because they could perform! So, it wasn't in the school's best interest to tell me Tupac may not graduate on time. You hear me?"

I nod yes.

"If he stays another year it benefits *them!* But I should have been more involved despite their efforts to keep me out of the loop."

I know what Afeni is talking about. I went to a performing arts high school, too. Good performers, like good athletes, become mascots for their schools—despite their credits, grades, or other credentials they need to graduate.

Afeni continues. "Anyway, Sekyiwa had been at Asante's over the summer and was going to school and everything was cool. Or so I thought. Meanwhile, I was saving money in Baltimore so Tupac and I could join her in like six months." Afeni shakes her head like "Ain't life a bitch?"

"Well, one day in October she calls me at work and tells me I better come get the kids 'cause she's going into rehab and her children and mine will be placed in foster care if I don't come out there immediately. Well, I wasn't ready to go out there. I didn't have money, but hey, I had to go. That was my first clue, that conversation with Asante, as to what alcoholism really was. I knew Asante drank, but I never associated nothing bad with it, 'cause everybody I knew drank. She made me understand, before that call was over, what alcoholism was all about because she was desperate and crazed, and I knew she was out of control.

"I gave my stuff away to anybody who wanted it, packed the rest of my shit up in two big suitcases, and took a bus to Marin City. Before I got to Asante's neighborhood, the bus broke down beneath an underpass. So I had to take a cab the rest of the way.

"When I got to Asante's apartment," Afeni proceeds, "everybody was gone. But there was a note on the door from Sekyiwa. It took me days to get to California, and Asante just left the kids with a neighbor. Set had sense enough to tell me where they were in her note. Asante's neighbors helped me get in Asante's apartment, helped me get situated, and bring some normalcy back to their lives. They all loved Set and told me how sweet she was." A cloud passes over Afeni's eyes and she is dark.

"This is when I heard horror stories. I found out how much my kids had endured. About how Asante would be drunk and look over at Tupac and just curse him out. All that bitterness, that resentment she had she would spit out at Tupac like he was her man and Sekyiwa got it every day: the screaming, the cursing. There was nothing she could do right. Asante was a mean, hateful drunk. She'd black out anywhere, legs open, mouth open—anywhere. Passed out for hours. When she came to, she didn't remember shit. My kids could not forgive her for what she had said." Afeni shakes her head slowly back and forth, then she resumes.

"My dilemma, at the time, as their mother, was that Sekyiwa *hated* Asante. She said it. She meant it and in due respect to Sekyiwa's feelings, I believed she did. You cannot stay in a person's home you despise. So, we had to get up out of there.

"You can't hate somebody and live off 'em, too. So another move." I need some coffee. This cold weak tea isn't doing it for me.

Afeni goes on to explain that Tupac stayed with some of his friends while she applied for a hardship case apartment and got one within a few months.

I am thinking about how much of a difference it would've made if there were daddies around. What would their life have been like had Mutulu been there for them in Baltimore? Instead, Mutulu Shakur, Sekyiwa's daddy, is in jail. Tupac is sixteen years old and Mutulu is the only father he has ever known, though Mutulu is not his biological father. Tupac does not know who the *sperm donor* is, and only relates to the men in his life who are there for him and his mother.

"So, it's just you, Afeni?" I ask her. "Everybody's gone? Where is Glo? Where are your friends? Why are you alone?"

She seems angry again, like I don't understand. But I understand, all right. I hear meanings insinuate themselves between the lines. Afeni doesn't want to come right out and acknowledge. I hear the drone of her missing sister.

"Glo's in New York and Tupac's grown. He's doing his

thing, and he's serious about it." Afeni puts out her cigarette and uncrosses her legs. Her stretched-out posture lets me know we are going to the next chapter. She has taken time to bring me up to speed. Now she's ready to tell me some shit.

"Cochise would tell Sekyiwa that he wanted me to meet Hassan, one of his jail buddies, when I came to town. Finally, I did."

"Oh, *Blind Date*," I mumble facetiously, referring to this whack reality-based TV show in L.A. that hooks utter strangers up in the most conspicuous sites and expects them to do the nasty.

Afeni ignores me. She knows I can't relate, and she knows I'm a smart ass. She doesn't have time for my sarcasm right now. She has a story to tell.

"I talked to Hassan on the phone, you know, one of those collect prison calls. Then, whenever I would visit Cochise, I would hook up with Hassan, too. Cochise was my friend. I loved him. He is godfather to my kids. So, just me hooking up with Hassan was also a favor to Cochise."

Ironic that my one experience at a jail was visiting Tupac at Dannemora prison on September 2, 1995. It was dreary and dreadful. Unlike me, the other visitors knew exactly what to do and exactly what to expect. I only went because he asked me to. He told his mom he wanted me to visit him. But for myself, that was an experience I could have done without. I knew after seeing Tupac in there, that he would not last long incarcerated. He was a wild stallion just playing the game for a little while before he cut loose.

Afeni cuts my painful memory short. "Hassan wrote me love letters, I remember that," Afeni goes on about her newfound companion. "I went to visit him around Thanksgiving. Then I kept going back to see him. And one visit, he keeps beggin' for pussy, like they all do, and I always said no. But this one time, for some reason . . ."

When Afeni says "one time," I am riveted. I know this is the beginning of the *one-time story* she promised to tell.

"He looks at me, and he was a tall and fine, beautiful young brother. 'Go into the bathroom,' he says. 'You go first. I'll come in right behind you.' And for some reason, I did it. We were in the bathroom for all of five seconds. Long enough for me to pull my pants down . . . and for him to stick it in and pump up and down. And that was it."

I see Afeni leaning on the cold white sink of the penitentiary restroom. Dirty tiles at her feet, balls of brown paper . . . I watch "her man" push it in her hard. She probably thought, "Just get it over with." We can all detach from a despicable situation for a few moments—even without drugs.

"And guess what?" Afeni glares at me, her lips are tight but her eyes still glisten in the streetlight. "I got pregnant."

I am staggered by her revelation. Still I try to work the math, to compute how old Afeni is by now. Tupac is sixteen. Sekyiwa twelve . . . She must be thirty-nine or forty.

"Here I am, trying to save the day. Getting my kids situated and Asante's children, too. Settling into my little subsidized apartment, and I find out I'm pregnant. And when I told Hassan, he was ecstatic! Like: 'Yippee! We're gonna have a fuckin' baby!'" Afeni is lost in the awe of how ludicrous this all was.

"He asked me to marry him. Gave me a ring he had made up by the jail's metal shop. My daughter took that ring and wore it for a long time before I snatched it back so no one could see it or know about it."

I see young Set trying to have a daddy, trying to handpick someone nice for her mommy. Someone for her family that won't get in the way. I can understand young Sekyiwa. She was trying to fix things.

"I got swept up in that shit. I took the blood test. He had the papers drawn up for my name change. He had his lawyer bring me some money to buy stuff. You know, furniture, a phone for my new apartment. He also had me bringing him drugs into the prison. That really bothered me. I found out later that's what I was really for, but it really fucked with me even then."

"Because you knew better," I say. "You knew the game!" She was being used! I reluctantly hear this life lesson: If Afeni can be used, *anyone* can be used. Because this is no stupid woman, and this woman has street smarts, life experience. She has been on drugs and in recovery, worked a nine-to-five, been on welfare. She's got a boy child and a girl child. She's been in prison. What does this boy, Hassan, know that Afeni doesn't know? And that's what hurts the worst. Nothing. Not a goddamn thing.

Miki Howard's seemingly benign song runs through my head—*Ain't nobody like you . . . I've been up and I've been down.* Afeni keeps talking. *I've had my feet swept off the ground. . . .* "Cochise had a visiting day. I went. Really, to see Hassan." *By somebody who just picked me up.* "And Cochise blocked the door when I got to the visiting room. Blocked me from going in because Hassan was in there, with a visit—from his other woman." *By somebody who just picked me up and threw me away. . . .* "His other woman who really was his real woman. And Cochise knew all the time. Knew all along and he treated me like a piece of shit." *I've been rich and I've been poor. I've had boys in and out my door. . . .* "Like a bitch on the street, Cochise was blockin' me from seein' the truth and I didn't forgive him for that for a long time. In fact, it took the kids, me and Asante's kids, for me to forgive Cochise."

Afeni starts to cry and I say, "Afeni, we've all been used. You ain't the only smart little bitch that someone used up for their own designs."

"I know. I know," she chokes out. "But this, this was the only thing I said I would never do. Fuck a man behind bars—and I did it! And it was raining that day, very hard. I took a cab back from San Quentin, and it cost me twenty something dollars." The tears, the snot, drip down her face. "And that was me crying in the rain, like the stupid bitch I was." Afeni blows her nose in a tissue. I learned not to pack up my Kleenex boxes but keep them close to Afeni. "There's nothing *worse* than being played by a nigga in jail.

All I could think was 'You's a stupid bitch. About the stupidest bitch that ever lived . . . ' And I believed it."

I realize now that this is really the first time Afeni really believes she is shit. Not when that boy from her school, Byron Cohen, called her a creature from another planet. Not when her daddy beat her mama's ass. Not when white boys called her a "black bald-headed bitch." Not when the police broke her door down and stuck a gun in her face. But this day and the days and months after, when she carried her "plantation baby," slowly killed her spirit.

"What happened after that was I hated myself . . . bad. And all I wanted was an abortion. The first time I went for an abortion they discovered my fibroids were sitting too big and in a bad place where they didn't feel safe doing an abortion. They didn't want to do it there. I was three months pregnant. They sent me to a different office, and that upset me greatly."

"You just wanted it over with," I say.

"Two strokes! And I got to deal with this shit for the rest of my life? How is that fair?"

I cannot answer Afeni, as I'm a bit surprised at how torn she is about having an abortion. I thought she would have done it immediately once reality kicked in: her age, her finances, her lack of support, her inability to care for another child. Why was she even going through the motions? I want to shake her the way you shake sense into hysterical people. Before I can do so, she continues:

"I was crazy, I told you. Could I have been thinking

right in any way? I waited so late because that's when I found that motherfucker with his other woman, his *real* woman." Afeni tosses the next line to me in a sober, hardened tone. "She was pregnant, too, by the way."

"What is going on? Why a man in jail?"

"There are so few men. It's not good for us to pretend that the statistics don't affect us individual women. Sister Souljah talks about this so well. All of us Black women as a whole suffer from not having a man, not just me. I thought it was because I had short hair, and I was dark—you know, that's what you go back to. I wanted it to be that reason. But the real situation is, there aren't that many men."

Afeni goes on. "So nobody would give me this damn abortion. One doctor passed me on to someone else. Then I'd be waiting, you know. These are clinics and nobody wants to do it, and now I'm five months and I'm desperate. I'm so rebellious with God . . . I can't make peace with this."

Five months. I think about one of my close friends losing her baby at five months. The heartache. The miscarriage. The formed fetus with dark hair and a button nose. She named her baby Camille.

"So I try to kill the baby myself," Afeni says. "I knew from my work at Legal Services that crack kills babies, so I started smoking crack. Every day, twenty-four-seven. I would get high and I'd feel the baby kick. Right in the beginning I'd feel it kick. I would just keep smokin' until it stopped kicking. Every day. Every day. But the baby wouldn't die. I wouldn't miscarry, and I hated that baby, and I hated myself for hating that baby."

"So much hate." My throat is tight, my words are dry.

"So much hate."

The night comes to a steel-blue color as the sun tries to rise.

"Did you call Glo?"

"Glo was freakin' out. She was scared I was too far gone in the pregnancy. She offered to keep the baby." Afeni stares at my grand piano even though it's clear that she does not see it. "But I know at a certain point, I'd have to *see* that baby even if Glo kept it. So I told her no. She didn't want me to be alone. She knew I was going to kill that baby no matter what she said, and I finally found a doctor that would. But she didn't want me to be alone. So I asked a neighbor, an older woman next door, to take me to my appointments. Back then it was a two-day procedure. Because I was five months, they did ultrasounds, and I actually saw that baby. She was long-legged in the womb. She was going to be tall."

I try not to cry too loud so Afeni can remember in peace, but I feel a sob break through from my gut for all discarded babies. The ones in the Dumpsters, the ones on the curb, and the ones that live only to be beaten and burned by cigarette butts and dumped in an alley. Please, make this story be over.

She continues. "I was anemic. They gave me iron pills and told me to take the maximum overnight. When I went back, my blood count was just high enough. Asante took me the last day. The woman who was taking me to the other appointments said she couldn't take me no more. She said God was trying to tell me something. Asante, on the other hand, was drunk. She could barely walk, but she took me to my abortion. We stayed up all night before. I don't know how we made it. But even in her drunken stupor, Asante knew that I had to go. When they put that needle in my stomach, before they knocked me out, I had labor pains. I had to deliver the baby. The needle was to stop the heartbeat of the fetus. Big long needle stuck in the belly. I know what I did and take responsibility for that. I saw that baby. I take responsibility for what I did. It was bad. And that baby died. And I was hooked on crack."

"I'm listening, Afeni." I put my hand over hers, as she struggles to spit the next part out.

"I had to tell my children that I was pregnant from this man in prison and that was the most humiliating thing, because how could I be pregnant from him? You had to visualize how I got pregnant. All the important things to me I had destroyed. There aren't that many men, and the ones in prison say the right things. There's a whole business in prison with men who know how to do it. They write letters for you. Hassan used to write letters for men. It has nothing to do with normal relationships, love and all that. Nothing to do with that and everything to do with survival."

I feel like it's happening all over again for Afeni, right

now in my apartment in the spill of the streetlight, in the rise of the sun, in the shadows cast by the towers of boxes in my living room.

Quiet dawn surrounds us and I keep silent until Afeni's breathing deepens. She is asleep. Time goes by, maybe an hour, because the garbage trucks clank outside on their morning pickup. I'm tired and I'm swollen from crying so much. She has told her story one time. The story that changed the course of her life forever. Now it's time to be still and let the baby rest.

SEVEN

Song of Sekyiwa

*"My mother said Tupac was her soul mate
and my life reflects that."*
—SEKYIWA SHAKUR

Why is a one-time story told only one time? Because it is a story we yearn to delete from our history. One-time stories hurt more than the stories we tell over and over again. Our oft-repeated family stories can be painful, traumatic, colorful, and blasting—like the crossing of oceans, the losses of innocence, the deaths of our mothers, the diseases of our grandfathers, the affairs of our fathers, the incarcerations of our sons. We pass these stories down from aunt to nephew; mother to child; father to son; and tell them just often enough to keep them alive. But a one-time story is better dead, and that is the difference. The pain is different in the one-time story because at its core there is humility and remorse. The one-time story hurts more because deep in the pit of the truth lies the realization that it was all your fault and the harm can never be undone. But the record must be set straight, so now I know I must go to Sekyiwa's for the other one-time stories Afeni will not tell me now, the one-time stories she will share only with her daughter, just as I will one day share mine with mine.

It has been months since Afeni shared her abortion story with me, but I would like to know how this incident affected her daughter. Afeni seems relieved when I tell her I'm going to spend some time with Sekyiwa.

"Yes, go. She's waiting for you." Afeni smiles broadly. "You must see Sekyiwa's house. She's doing well. And, she did this all by herself."

I kiss Afeni good-bye and drive the three or four minutes to Sekyiwa's house. Glo and Tommy, Set and her two children, and Glo's daughter Jamala and her daughter Imani, all have homes within a five-mile radius in Stone Mountain. It's like a commune, everyone floating easily from house to house while knowing they have separate corners of retreat.

Set's house is contemporary but warm, with hardwood floors. Antique-framed family photos adorn the mantel. Shona sculptures made of soapstone and Ashanti fertility statues people the corners of her living room. African art and paintings splash colors along the walls, and I instantly feel at home. I see a joy celebrated in her home, a joy of being African and being American, of being healthy and young, and I can't believe this is a child who once wanted to commit suicide. I don't want to bring this up first to Sekyiwa, but it is foremost in my mind. As if she knows this to be true and not being one to ignore the elephant in the middle of the family room, she starts off with her new-found peace. She attributes her sanity with the treatment she received at Sierra Tucson, a rehabilitation center in Arizona.

"Once I was diagnosed with post-traumatic stress syndrome, it all made sense. I could get help and learn how to help myself." Set says calmly.

"Post-traumatic stress syndrome," I repeat, more for myself. "What are the symptoms? I mean, that's what Vietnam vets suffer from and people who survived 9/11."

"I know," she says. "PTSD is something we don't always see right away because something else is going on. Like for me, I was depressed and suicidal. I had these fits of rage. But to know I am a trauma survivor has helped me get help and treatment."

"With a name and diagnosis you know what to do."

"Yes, and I want to thank you for reaching out to me when you did. You said things that meant a lot to me. Especially coming from you. You know, *Jasmine Guy*."

Unfortunately, at this point, I *don't* know what Set's talking about. I feel a tiny quiver of panic as I try to remember something I may have said to her that affected her so deeply. Shit, I hate this feeling. It's like the many times in my life when I can't remember someone's name. Someone I met before but don't know how or when or what to call them.

Sekyiwa's laugh interrupts me. "You don't remember, do you?" she exclaims, watching my confusion. She is incredulous that something so important to *her* could have slipped *my* mind.

I try to fudge. "Well, not verbatim," I say. " I mean, I know I talked to you about school and work and Nzingha's future and learning how to help yourself and take care of your needs but—"

Sekyiwa laughs again. "You're a trip," she observes. "You still don't know who you are."

"Now what does that mean?" I ask.

"You still don't know you're Jasmine Guy," she responds.

"Well, thank you for clarifying that."

She continues. "You don't know how you affect people."

"I did what was natural for me to do," I say. "All I know is, you were on the periphery, Set. When I first saw you, you had a little baby. You were nineteen, and your eyes were big, brown, and beautiful. You looked like a little kid trying to be strong, trying to hang with this state of emergency your family was in. But *you* needed normalcy and comfort, diapers and peace. That's what you needed. And, instead, you were surrounded by chaos and despair. Your brother had been shot five times. He could have died and there you were with your new little baby.

"I reached out to you because nobody else did. It was a bad time." At that awful time, when Tupac was first shot, no one seemed to be there for Sekyiwa, and everyone seemed justified in ignoring her. Tupac was shot, and he was their lifeline. All energies channeled to him, and Set did what she could.

Sekyiwa goes on: "You started talking about feeling bad about yourself, and what you were like at my age. You told me stories about being alone in New York, about being a dancer and feeling fat, about being lonely and making bad choices, and how you didn't like yourself very much." She starts to smile and laughs a little. "I couldn't believe it. 'Cause when I looked at you, especially then, it was like a whole 'nother thing I saw because I didn't think you would have problems like *me*. You were different. You were light-skinned for one, and famous and all. I just couldn't believe we really had things in common, like bad things."

"Yeah, we were equally messed up!" We laugh. "It was easy to reach out to you. You're easy to talk to."

"You are, too. And you should know that," she says, soberly. "You should know the good things about who you are, not just the fucked-up things."

I'm uncomfortable with Set talking about me, pointing out so clearly the things I have always known about myself. This shift in conversation from Sekyiwa and her problems to me and my battle with perspective keeps me quiet for a moment. Sekyiwa smiles, a bit smug. She seems amused that I could be so old and still so mistaken about my true self.

I give in and provide some explanation. "I'm sure it happened early," I tell Set. "My perspective, my self-image. You know, I developed it a long time ago. And the way I see myself is always worse than it really is, but that is *my* reality."

"That's what you *think* your reality is," she corrects me.

"Right. Whatever." Damn, she was really listening at Sierra Tucson. I don't feel like being analyzed right now, nor am I sure it would do any good. I don't want to express my doubts about analysis to Set where counseling and reflection have obviously helped her.

"The closer I get to Afeni, the more I realize how much she is like my mother," I tell Set.

"For real?" Set is surprised. I guess my mom and hers don't seem to have much in common on the outside.

"Yeah. They are both tough and straight-talking. They are opinionated and stubborn. It's easy to talk to them about things people find shocking or deplorable."

"Well, she may be easy for *you* to talk to. . . . And other people, you know, act like she's this guru or something, but she's my mother to me."

"Yeah, even that!" I agree. "Everyone talks to my mother: her students, her nieces. She always had stray cats—that's what I call my mother's other children. Kids that loved her and needed her and were always at the house. Kids that wished they had a mother like my mother instead of what they had."

"And if they had been her real children like you and Monica were, it would have been a whole other story. Like what *I* needed from my mom she couldn't give me. I needed hugs, kisses. My mom isn't like that."

"That's funny," I say, "because Afeni's very warm with me, affectionate, and supportive. That's weird."

"That's what I'm talking about!" Sekyiwa looks at me, wide-eyed. "I see it with my own daughter. She's all over me sometimes. 'Mommy, you're pretty.' 'I like your hair, Mommy.' And it gets on my nerves! I know she needs some affection, some loving, some attention—"

"But you don't want her to need it. It scares you. Just like it scared our mothers."

"Nzingha is just like I was, real sweet. She does OK in school, but she's not real, real smart like my mother and my brother. She's not an intellectual. She's more like me."

"And do you try to toughen her up?" I can't help but wonder.

"Yeah. I try not to snap at her, but it's hard because I don't want her to be so needy, so gushy."

"She's soft," I say.

"Yeah." Set agrees.

"And that scares you." I smile. I'm reminded of a whipping my sister got when we were little. "Monica and I walked to school every day down this big ol' hill. After school we walked back up the hill, sometimes with other kids. This one day, a little girl in Monica's class was walking with us and she kept pushing Monica and punching her in the back. So I grabbed the little girl by her collar—"

"How old were you?"

"Fifth grade. I was nine. Monica was six, second grade. I told the girl that if she didn't stop hitting Monica, 'her head would be bleeding on the cement,' and she left her alone. But the little girl had a big sister in sixth grade. By the end of the next day, the whole sixth grade was going to beat my ass. My teacher was so freaked out, she drove me and Monica home.

"My mother got to the bottom of the story and found out Monica had stolen the little girl's candy or something, and that's why the little girl was pushing on her. My mother was so pissed. She whipped Monica with the belt, and I listened from the other room, crying. It was horrible. I just wanted her to stop."

"I used to cry when Tupac got whipped. Then my mother would spank me for crying for him, and Tupac would laugh at me."

"Damn."

"Well, I know you didn't come here to talk about me." Sekyiwa gets up. "You want some ice tea?"

"Do you have Coke? I just want to hear your side of things, Set. Your voice is missing in Afeni's story."

From the kitchen she tells me. "I'm not really comfortable talking about her life. It feels like I'm betraying secrets, but my mom said it was all right." She sits in a leather recliner and hands me my drink.

"I just really need to know what happened once Afeni started doing crack. What happened to you? I just need to know about the things your mother won't tell me."

Set looks grown-up today, confident.

"Why won't she tell you?" Set asks me knowing that Afeni and I talk about most everything.

"Because they are *your* things, and she doesn't feel she has the right." Set understands and nods her head. "So, I may not know things you think I know."

"You knew about me being in the hospital, didn't you?" Sekyiwa sits down across from me in her leather recliner. "You knew I tried to commit suicide, right?"

"Yes, but I'm just not sure why or what led up to that."

"I was so tired of hurting. My chest was so tired. I was so tired of my chest feeling like that, and I remember that pain from childhood, since I was a baby. . . . I called Malcolm, since he knew me all my life. We grew up together. We had our children together. I called him 'cause we were close. 'Why am I so sad?' I asked him. 'Because your brother died,' he told me. 'But I was sad before that,' I said to him. And he said, 'You were? I thought you were just crazy.'"

"Crazy?"

"Yeah, my family just thought I was crazy. And I acted crazy at times. I was so angry, so enraged. I would scream and throw things and hurt people. And even the last time, before I went into the hospital, I called my mother, and I asked her what was wrong with me. I asked her why I was so sad and if she knew anybody who was always sad! I begged her to tell me the truth. Was I one of these people who was always weak and always needy and will I always be sad?"

This is the phone call Afeni told me about months ago, the phone call she said she was glad she could take. She had received it sober and alert, but she had no answers for her child.

Sekyiwa continues: "'Do these sad people ever live happily?' I ask Mom. 'Can I call them and talk to them? Because I can't live like this, in this pain anymore.' I didn't want to be a strong Black woman. I didn't want to be *Dear Mama*. I didn't want to be Glo, just livin' for my kids. I didn't want to be Aunt Jemima. I was lost and so unhappy. My life added up to nothing."

This is a sad and horrifying revelation. Still, I find myself impressed by her ability to lash out and explode. I always implode.

"I was pissed off at Tupac," Set goes on, "because *I* was the one who was gonna kill myself . . . And then *he* died. . . . So I couldn't even do that.

"I called my father [Mutulu Shakur] and I screamed: 'You better send me to some war in Africa with whatever connections you have, because I need to do something with this rage. I need to be on the front lines killing somebody or I'm gonna kill people here or kill myself.' I spent the rest of the time on the couch with a gun under my chest."

"You were *really* going to kill yourself, Sekyiwa?"

"Death was all around me. The son of a close friend of my mom's committed suicide, you know. Another cousin of mine in Baltimore killed himself. Yafeu, my cousin—dead. Tupac—dead. It was no big thing to me to think about dying. It had to be better than living in rage, living in pain like this sadness. I talked to them in my living room—Yafeu, Tupac, and God, as if they were still alive right there with me. Yafeu, who was like a brother to me, told me he wouldn't leave; he did. I told Tupac he wasn't shit because he always left me behind, and then I felt Tupac go like this—" She raises her hand and shoots the finger. "As if he was saying fuck it; like, leave it alone Sekyiwa, and I did.

"I didn't kill myself that day because God had turned his back on me and I was afraid I would go to hell. I didn't want to die and go to hell. So I found my way to Sierra Tucson and got some help."

"You got left a lot, huh, Sekyiwa—dumped." I'm feeling sad for the little girl who's now a woman and mother of two. "I'm surprised you didn't do drugs. It was all around you."

"No. Asante cured me of alcoholism—watching her drunk and mean and passed out, and my mom kept me from cocaine. I never want to be like them. I remember I tried reefer once. I told my mom, and she was like, 'That's good, baby, you need something to relax you,' and I said, 'Hell, no. I'll never do that shit again.' It was like a movie when your whole life flashes before your eyes. I saw myself as a crackhead. No, they kept me away from all that shit, but I did other things." Evidently, addiction did not escape her completely. "My thing was sex. I had it early. . . . I had sex a lot from twelve to fourteen."

"That was the same time Afeni was using."

"Yes. I never saw her do it, though. She was never around me high, but I knew. I would find stuff in her purse—pipes and paraphernalia—and I would throw them out. One time, I called her over Charlene's house, and me and my mom were talking. Then all of a sudden, Charlene was on the phone with me and I knew someone had passed my mother the pipe. She just got off the phone—no 'hold on' or good-bye or nothing."

"Charlene," I repeat halfway to myself. I know Charlene from Afeni's stories about her. "Afeni told me she was the only person she knew that smoked crack all day and still wasn't skinny. Charlene had money and a nice apartment, so the people who couldn't afford to be seen smoking crack, professionals, teachers and what not, would smoke it right there at Charlene's, till all hours."

I remember Afeni's stories about Charlene because she was setting me straight about me saying she was homeless while she was on crack. I guess I assumed she was homeless or had heard Afeni was homeless while she was using, but that part of the urban legend was not true.

"In fact, she lived in an apartment with some guy who made seven hundred dollars a week, and they pay the rent with part of it and smoke up the rest. The rest of the time she spent at Charlene's.

"When my mom was cracked out, she'd be gone for

months," Sekyiwa says. "But I would pretend she was around so they couldn't take me away like to a home or something; I still went to school and everything. One day I was playing double Dutch, and I twisted my ankle. I remember saying to the other kids, 'I will tell my mother, and she will help me.' I was limping for a week before my mother came home to check on me. And I was happy to see her. We had a nice evening, and then she started talking about Nonburb Lane—a group home for kids. I cussed her out. I told her 'I am paying the rent. I am taking care of myself, so why do *I* have to go *away*? You're the fucking crackhead!' I told her. 'You go away!' And she did. Back to her crackhhead boyfriend and Charlene.

"Oooo, I cussed her out so bad. Because here I am alone in the eighth grade. Tupac's living with friends and working with Digital Underground. My mom's gone and doing crack. Asante's in rehab. Her kids are with her family, and I am alone. I do what I can do. Then she pops in out of nowhere and tries to be my mother? Tries to make some decisions for me?"

"Did you have a job? How were you eating or paying the rent?" I ask her. "I don't understand how people live without work."

"I had a boyfriend. He sold drugs. He'd give me money or he'd give me some reefer to sell. Eventually he moved in with me."

"Damn. How old was he?"

"Twenty-three."

"And *you* had an apartment and *he* didn't?" This is some crazy shit to me.

"See, after we left Asante's my mom applied for a subsidized apartment. So I stayed there with him, and he paid our five-dollar rent when my mom was delinquent. I almost got evicted once, and he paid it 'cause my mother wasn't around."

"No wonder you were enraged."

Sekyiwa says softly, "I was filled with rage, but it would just come out in these fits. When I would go off, I couldn't control it. I couldn't stop it once it started. . . . Everyone just thought I was crazy."

"But now you know you're not." I bring her back to the present. "Now you are here and a mother of two who can learn from your pain but not have to relive it."

"Yeah," says Sekyiwa, a little revived and in much more the tone I found her in at the start of our conversation. "I love Sierra Tucson. It changed my life. Tupac would have loved it, too. It could have helped him so much."

"Would he have gone?" I ask doubtfully.

"I don't know, but he would have stayed once he got there." She uncrosses her legs in the big leather chair and leans forward elbow to knee. "We had a sad childhood, Jasmine. He died before we could work everything out. Like if we had gone on to be, you know, thirty-five and thirty. Where we could look back on shit and fix it or laugh about it or, I don't know, apologize for things we had done to each other. Like you and Monica, like Glo and Afeni." Her eyes glaze over, but she doesn't cry. "But we didn't have that time."

"I'm so sorry you lost your brother," I say, and I do cry, because I had not cried for Sekyiwa, yet, and it was time. "I'm so sorry you miss out on having him as you grow up, and that your babies won't know their uncle."

She smiles at me and says, "Thank you. I have my mother, though, and we've gotten a lot closer. I feel like she understands me better."

"She's more accepting," I tell her. "And she's proud of you, Sekyiwa. She's proud of the woman you've become without her teaching you to be."

"She thinks she hasn't taught me to be the woman I've become?" Sekyiwa acts like that's ridiculous.

"Well, that's what she thinks." I shrug. "She doesn't claim the good, but the bad is glaring. That's another trait she and my mother have in common. Maybe it's a mother thing. But it's clear to me that we both got the good stuff, too. You are strong and clear and on your way when you could have died many times. That to me is Afeni. She always gets back up."

"I was never like her and Tupac. You know, intellectual, political—"

"Charismatic," I add.

"Loud," she laughs. "I just wanted her to be able to love me anyway even though I wasn't like her. Now, I feel she does."

I walk over to the baby pictures of Sekyiwa's children

on the mantel. In the middle of their photos is an older framed picture of Sekyiwa at seven. She's smiling, and the plaits sticking out of the side of her head have bowed ribbons at the top.

"You're her baby girl," I say. "She wants to rise to the honor of being your mother."

EIGHT

Redemption

"But children, I submit, cannot be fooled.
They can only be betrayed by adults...."
—James Baldwin

Hours later I'm back at Afeni's. It's dark now in Stone Mountain, and the air is warm and wet. I'm grateful for the meshed screen surrounding the porch at this time because Afeni and I can be outside without being eaten alive by gnats and mosquitoes. I love the calm of warm East Coast nights. Nights are cold on the West Coast no matter what time of year, and I am still not used to the sudden drop in temperatures that nightfall brings in L.A.

Afeni doesn't ask what I talked about with Sekyiwa. She just wants to know if the conversation went well, and if I got information for the book.

"She helped to fill in some blanks for me during your Marin City time . . . when you were using," I explain as I open a bottle of Becks. "Sorry," I say and nod to the Becks. "This is a lot for me to hear at once."

Afeni laughs a little. "I know," she says. "See, *I* knew what you were getting into." She laughs a little more. "*You* didn't!"

Her laugh is hearty, and I smile while she gets a kick out of my emotional exhaustion. "I don't know how therapists do this shit all day long," I say. "Just listening to fucked-up stories over and over. I am whupped. . . ." I sip my beer. "But I am also inspired by the resilience of the human spirit. It's a fragile resilience, though. It seems like we are always on the edge of just not making it."

"That's why I tell you, your job is to take care of your daughter. If you can do that right there, you are fulfilling your duty. I left Sekyiwa at a critical point in her life. At the time in her life she was developing into a woman, a time in her life when she was maturing and needed me there. Tupac was different. Of course, my addiction affected him, but he was off doing his career like a madman. He was obsessed."

"He had nothing else to lean on," I say. Everyone was leaning on him, I think.

"I know. I'm just saying that he didn't *need* me like Sekyiwa did because he was older. He was seventeen and eighteen years old. He was already out of the house. Set was thirteen and fourteen years old, a crucial time for her growing up. . . . Then she got pregnant."

Afeni grabs her cigarettes and leans forward to light up. She sits with her legs crossed underneath her and her elbow rests on her knees. She begins to pull in the menthol smoke and it drifts over the view of the dark woods like a foggy mist. "We all have issues due to abandonment. My daddy left me. Their daddies left them . . . and then I left them."

I look at the clouded tree trunks lit by the floodlights on the side of the house. "You can abandon someone and still be in the room," I tell her.

"Yes, and I probably neglected them at times even before I used, but once I picked up the pipe, I left for real. And if I hadn't done *crack*, if it had been any other drug, I'd probably still be using. But *crack*, that drug right there, does nothing but make you want it more. Crack takes over, and I told you I liked cocaine. That was my drug of choice—not alcohol, not heroin, not anything else. All that other shit I could do and put down, but crack—"

"But that's why you thought you could do it, right? Your history had always been controlled using of cocaine. And then you met a drug you couldn't control."

"And it kicked my ass," Afeni concludes.

"Well, you seem like you needed an ass-whuppin' every now and then." I try to joke, knowing she has had more than her share of ass-whuppin's.

"I told you," she laughs, "that's why Glynn Turman hauled off and slapped me that day!"

"Stop tellin' me that. It's disturbing," I protest as Afeni

laughs some more. "I'm not talking about that kind of ass-whuppin!"

"I know, I know." Afeni breathes again.

She reminds me of Tupac right now. He laughed like Afeni, freely and deeply. They laugh from their gut and it sounds good. I remember them all laughing together—Glo, Afeni, Tupac, Sekyiwa, and it was loud and warm and infectious. They could laugh in the middle of chaos, because chaos always caught up with them.

"You managed to stay together. There is still a lot of love in your family in spite of drugs, abandonment, and poverty," I remind Afeni. "Nobody stayed mad or stayed gone too long. But that anger is strong when it comes."

"Yeah, it simmers then explodes. We all got that, me and my kids. We express it in different ways. Thank God, Tupac had his music and his art. Because he was through with me when I was using." Afeni lives it again for a moment. "And he should have been. Shit. It was 1990 and I had come down to Marin City to see Tupac. Because by this time, I lost my apartment and was living with this man. I was so poor, and I had no money except when the man got his money and we used that on drugs."

Afeni never names her lovers. They just become one big generic "man"—*this* man, or *the* man. I have to assume the man she refers to now is the same "man" Afeni went to Lake Tahoe with when she left Sekyiwa in Marin City. "Tupac had been to Japan with Digital Underground and I went to see him. He gave me some money that day," she continues. "I remember him going in his pocket and peeling money off a big wad. . . . I may have bought *food* with it because I was so ashamed. I couldn't use it on crack. I would hear about Tupac coming through or being on TV and stuff like that, but we were not in direct communication."

"He was ashamed of you."

"I would bring him down, and he couldn't afford that. He was our only way out. So he couldn't deal with me high and fucked up.

I remember once I had gotten very, very sick and talked to him on the phone. I tried to get him to come see me, and he was like, 'What can I do?' He was very cold. I was so hot with fever that I crawled down to the lady downstairs, and when she opened the door, she could feel the heat from my body. I crawled down there to get money to go to the hospital and I think she actually took me there. They gave me antibiotics, the fever went down, and I was okay. Then Thanksgiving came. Those two things really made me look at, really look at where I was. It wasn't about my children because my daughter was safe in New York with Glo, and my son was safe out on his own. It was really *me* who was not safe. I was dying, and I knew that I was dying because my spirit was not there at all. I would go to bed at night and really not care whether or not I woke up. Something inside of me was pushing me to get home, get to New York and my family. I was on an insane, desperate mission to make it back home."

"Even if it was to die at home . . ."

"Especially if it was to die. I wanted to die home with my family, not alone in Marin County. So Tommy, Glo's husband, sent me some money for a bus ticket. Me and the guy smoked that right up."

"As desperate as you were to get home, you smoked up your ticket money?" I ask.

"Hey, I'm an addict. I do as addicts do," Afeni says casually. "Tupac met me at the bus station—him and his friend Mike Cooley. Tupac reached in his pocket and gave me all the money that he had in his pocket. . . . Mike Cooley went in his pocket and gave me some money, too. . . . I ended up having about sixty dollars. And I got on the bus.

"It was one of those winters where it was really cold in the west. In northern California, where I was, we were waking up and water was thick, frozen. On the bus trip coming across you go through Nevada and Utah. Utah was the first place, right in the middle of nowhere, where the bus broke down. The first time it broke down, they had to call and send another bus to get the passengers. My feet, I still have trouble with my toes. So we got on the new bus they sent and we broke down another time. I developed a real love and appreciation for the Salvation Army because they were at the bus station in Denver, Colorado, with food, with hot soup and blankets and, you know, they were concerned because lots of people were getting stranded in buses everywhere all over the west."

"Damn, I never think about the Salvation Army doing stuff like that. They lived up to their name," I said.

"This was December . . . 1990. I always have to count back from my sobriety date to know the year things happened." She acknowledges her method of chronicling her life's events. "Yes. This was the first year of the bus strike also. So there weren't that many buses or drivers. I ran out of money at some point, probably in Wisconsin. I sat next to a white woman from Berkeley on the bus, and I remember concocting a story. . . . I started acting like my credit cards were in my bag packed underneath the bus and all like that, and she shared her food with me. That's basically how I ate coming halfway across the country."

"Your money from Tupac was gone," I say.

"Well, once I bought my ticket, yes. My family talked me home, for real. Every stop I called them crying, cold, hungry, alone. And they talked me home—my daughter, my nephew, Katari, the youngest one, he gave me strength over that phone. He told me he loved me, and he missed me, and he wanted me home."

Now Afeni cries, so moved by the love of her young nephew. When she says "my family" it's as if she says *God*. *God* talked me back home. I called *God* at every stop, and *God* talked me home.

"I got to Port Authority on Christmas Eve. I had five suitcases 'cause I had everything I owned. I called my family and told them I was there 'cause the bus was so off-schedule they had no idea when I would arrive. By the time my family finally got there, I can see myself right now. I was sitting on the floor at Port Authority against one of those pillars with all five of my bags around me. I could've weighed ninety-five pounds. When I saw my family come down the steps, it was the first time I felt human again. I had ceased to be or feel like a human being. I didn't know who I was anymore, or even who I used to be. I really didn't. So when I saw them it was like a signal that I belonged. I really did belong someplace, you know. And they loved me, gently, back to health. They took me home, and they loved me. I started to feel human again."

The power of their love is still palpable. They take care of each other always, these two sisters and their families. I remember that autumn day in '94 during the trial when I saw this same clan encircle Tupac with a wall of protection. They loved him back to himself. I remember him waiting in a wheelchair for his hearing to begin, and they surrounded him, just as they surrounded Afeni on Christmas Eve five years before when she sat broken on the floors of Port Authority. Again, Tupac's life mirrors Afeni's.

Afeni continues, "I think I must've gone and gotten on welfare, and when I got the welfare money I would give almost all of it to Glo and Tommy. I would keep a little bit. But whatever I kept, I would use to get high on. I would do that in the bathroom. . . . Tommy and Glo, mostly Tommy, had told me: 'You want to get high, you can get high, you can do anything you want, but you don't have to go outside. You don't have to be in the street.' Basically, I accepted that as a wonderful thing. I didn't really have to go out to get high. I could get high in the house, and that's what I did."

"Set said the grown-ups would all go to the bathroom together and how it would smell sweet, but like shit. And she thought you all had sweet-smelling shit." I laugh.

"I didn't like myself 'cause I was getting high with my nephew, Scott, and he was getting high badly then. When people get high they get ugly. So I didn't like myself any more than I had before; I wasn't feeling good going to bed. This was basically what was happening the first part of 1991. I was gaining a little weight, but I was still getting high."

Afeni's recovery is crucial to her story. In fact, I think it's the only reason she even wanted to write this book. Her road to recovery begins in the Port Authority that Christmas Eve in '90. She has five more months of smoking crack in her sister's apartment bathroom, five more months of sitting on the toilet and blowing it out the window, five more months of sucking on that pipe with her own nephew, Scott, until she finds AA. Or, I should say, AA finds her.

"It was the twentieth anniversary of the New York 21 acquittal. It was the weekend preceding May twelfth, which is my sober date. I didn't want to go but Ali Bey, who was one of the 21, and his wife, Sue, she just wore me down. She's one of those kind of white women that just talk you to death until you gave in. She came and picked me up from Glo's and brought me out to Connecticut." Afeni chuckles to herself and remembers how Sue's persistence got her to the anniversary.

"Why didn't you want to go to the anniversary?" I ask her. "You just rather stay holed up in Glo's place getting high?"

Afeni explains. "People knew me to be arrogant and disdainful, and basically that's what I was. You know, I blamed everyone for my problems. I held on to that anger. I believed that shit. . . . You know I did everything on my own. I'm bad and fuck ya'll. . . . That's where I was. That's how I felt about the Panthers."

"But you went."

"Yeah, I went because of fuckin' Sue. She did everything. She picked me up, drove me to Connecticut, and put me up in her house. I woke up the next day to the smell of hot coffee. Then I saw their daughter, Tonya, walk by the bedroom. I hadn't seen Tonya since she was a teenager, and she looked so good. I was so happy to see this girl. Tonya had been a child when her father got arrested. At sixteen she had had the metal of a cop's gun shoved into her face just because she lived in the same place as her dad. I was so happy to see her looking strong and secure, you know. This girl caught hell in her life. She had been on crack and alcohol, she had been abused, she lost two of her children. I'm telling you, *hell*. And here she was standing before me looking so good and peaceful. I remember saying to her. 'It's so good to see you. Where are you going this time of morning?' She says: 'Oh, I'm going to a meeting. You wanna go?' I said, 'Well, yeah,' because I didn't want to be staying there listening to Sue all day. And that's how I got to my first meeting, and I didn't know where I was going. I didn't fall on my knees and cry 'Help me.' I just went with Tonya."

"She was like an angel for you," I say.

Afeni smiles. "God looked down upon my stupid, simple ass, and it was literally his grace that saved me. It turned out that the meeting she was going to was, of course, an AA meeting, a recovery meeting at the hospital. I listened with my notebook open and I took notes on all that they were saying. They were talking about alcoholism, saying addiction was a disease. That's what the subject was. And they defined a disease and the characteristics of a disease. That was the first time that I heard that. I thought, oh, okay, let me see what this is.

"It was actually amazing to me, I mean, the people in there and how they were talking. This one girl, who had had so much trouble in her life, she had been abused as a child and ran away. She was homeless and had been raped. She went to that meeting. Then we went to the house of somebody who was in recovery, and we sat around and just talked. This woman just opened her house to us! This was all a new experience for me. I'm looking at the people . . . I think it's very nice that these are *normal* people who used to use drugs. They don't look like me. They got shoes on, nice stuff on. They're happy. This is all very interesting. . . .

Then, that night, we went to another meeting and it was at that meeting—"

I furrow my brow. "In the same day?"

"Oh, yes. Girl, it took me three meetings a day just to get a clue. First of all, I had to realize that I was like these people. Because I walked in thinking I was different. I was smarter for one thing, and I looked very different. I had my hair shaved off like Tupac did. I had on an orange dress and, really, I looked real different—"

"Hare, Hare, Hare." I chant a mock Hare Krishna song and laugh.

"Nah, more like something really weird . . . off of an Isaac Hayes album or something, 'cause I had the earrings on, too, and the nose ring. So, anyway, in that meeting the group sat in a semicircle. There was an inside circle and an outside circle. It was full, packed full, and there were about five other Black people. That was nice to see. I listened to what they had to say, because I thought maybe they would understand what was going on with me.

"Well, they start the meeting by saying: 'My name is so and so and I'm an addict.' The topic for tonight is whatever it was. They went around the room and you said your clean date and that you're an addict. Then you talk on the topic for a minute. By the time it got to me, I didn't say nothing but: 'My name is Afeni, and I'm just here.' But by the time the meeting was over, I knew I wasn't just 'here.' I was an addict. I felt like all of those people were in my head and knew my secrets. Every time one of them talked, they

talked about *me*. They described my own very special experiences, my feelings, my thoughts—everything."

Afeni glows right now as she remembers recovery. She
reminds me of Ingrid Bergman as Joan of Arc basking in
the light of her faith in God. In the lift of her cheekbones I
see happiness, a happiness that had not lived in the tales of
her past. This moment of recovery, of finding an answer, is
a transforming experience for Afeni. Afeni, who believes in
God and grew up in the sanctified Church, found her faith
in AA.

"I thought they had a big secret, though. I heard them
say get a sponsor. So I wanted to get one because a sponsor
would tell me the secret. I didn't know shit about what a
sponsor should do or what that relationship was all about.
I just thought they held the 'secret.'

"The first sponsor I got, I didn't choose very well. I just
chose somebody that was pretty, who was young and
vibrant and looked like she had it going on. But she was
not right. In fact, she ended up having a relationship with
my nephew, who was clean only three weeks."

"Hold up. . . . I thought in recovery you're not supposed
to be with anybody for a year." That was one fact I knew
from friends of mine who couldn't abstain.

"Yes. And my nephew's sponsor was telling him the
same thing—no relationships, no relationships. It was a
mess, but I went to a meeting that night and I stood up
and I said: 'I fired my sponsor. The person that I chose was
not helping me.' Nobody said anything to me right then.

You know they don't stop a meeting for anything. But at the *end* of the meeting people came up to me, people who had been recovered for a long time, and they knew that I was desperate. When they see somebody new come in to the room, they can feel when that person really wants to be sober, and they knew I wanted it. People were helpful to me that night. They gave me names of eligible sponsors. Everybody that gave me the names gave me the *same* three names.

"During the break I went up to the first woman that I recognized on that paper. It was Marian H., and I asked her if she would please be my sponsor. She asked me a few questions, and I started on my recovery. I started to learn the tools of recovery through her, and she was tough. She had lived the life, had been in the service, in the navy and an aerial photographer. She had lived a daring life, not a tulip garden all her life, and she never let me bullshit her."

"Well, that's what you needed. Who else would you have listened to?"

"No, she was the one. Because literally, I knew something had to change all the way inside of me, not superficially. I didn't know how I was gonna do it. I didn't think I could do it. I always thought they had this magical cure. I always thought that there was something at a certain point they would give me. I kept hearing these words and phrases."

"Like what?"

"Like 'let go.' A 'higher power.' 'Steps,' 'inventory,' 'day at a time,' 'let God remove,'" she rattles off the catch-phrases with ease. "One thing I was anxious to do was the fourth step. Your personal inventory. I wanted to do that shit and get it over with."

"Why?" A lot of this program sounds like pure hell to me.

"Because I had seen a lot of people go out because they hadn't done the fourth step. I saw a lot of people come in, and they would be so cute sitting in the center aisle. Then they'd go out and use drugs and try to come back again. All over the fourth step."

"What is inventory?"

"With your fourth step you write down all the things that you thought you'd take to the grave, and you share these things with your sponsor. Everything: resentments, mistakes, all of it. I couldn't wait to take those things off my chest. I couldn't wait to be free."

"What kind of things? Things that you did wrong? Bad things?" I'm thinking this is like a confession is for Catholics. Telling your worst shit to someone so you can be at peace. I remember confessing to my mom every night before I could go to sleep. I was six then, already taking inventory, though as life went on, I learned to keep things in, especially bad things.

"Why do you have to do this?" I ask Afeni. "Why do you have to tell your sponsor?"

"Because the thing that really drives our behavior is our secrets, the little things that we are hiding inside. We always have to do things in order to keep them hidden. Then you have layers and layers and layers of stuff on it, and it just keeps us sick. I listened to them talk about secrets and how keeping secrets made us sick inside. The basic thing in the fourth step is that you tell all that stuff. But the most important thing that you must do is tell that one thing that you're holding on to, that you promised you would tell no one. That's the thing you have to tell. I was afraid I wasn't gonna be able to be rigorously honest, but I did it like I was told. I did it in two days, in two sittings.

"My sponsor suggested that I go into a room. That I take into that room all liquids that I wanted to consume during an eight-hour period, any snacks or food I wanted to have. I needed to unplug the phone. I needed to not answer the door. I needed to do nothing but write on a piece of paper under the heading of Hidden Resentments. I needed to go back as far as I could remember. Start with the first resentment that I could remember as a child. I went and did all my *resentments* for those hours. The next day I did the same thing with my *faults*, things that I had done to other people. I put it on the paper and folded it up like I was asked to. I had to keep the paper and hold on to it until she made an appointment for us to do a fifth step.

"On the fifth step she took me to the park. She brought a picnic basket and we sat on the blanket, and she opened up my paper and she went over everything on the paper.

She didn't ask me to elaborate or explain anything away. She wrote down on another paper categories, about seven categories. Under each one she was making marks. By the time she got to the end, to the last one, she asked me if I had any issues around sexuality. I said I didn't think I did, and I told her my experiences and stuff like that. Then I found out what those seven categories were—"

"The seven deadly sins," I interject. "Gluttony, sloth . . ." I go through the gruesome murders in my head. "Greed, pride . . ." I go through the sins I remember. "Greed, pride—"

"That's the one that got me!" Afeni exclaims. "I got confused. When my sponsor told me that my greatest defects of character have been pride and anger, I realized I didn't understand what pride was. I thought that pride was good. I had lived my life being proud and thinking that proud was the best thing in the world for me to be. And there she was telling me that pride was kicking my butt, pride and anger. Anger I understood. I knew that's how I went into the party and that was really what was driving me.

"My first year clean and sober, my sponsor wrote me a card. I'll never forget it. Of course, I thought I had done it. Everybody loved me and I was Miss Fuckin' Recovery now. My sponsor spent a whole page on that card talking about how I'm in danger of my pride. Again, I couldn't get it. In fact, I thought that she was really being a little overfamiliar, you know. I think that was really my last hurdle to deal with—my pride. But I dealt with that when I had to deal with my children. Having to deal with my children in recovery is what brought me humility."

"How did they act when they saw that you were committed?"

"My daughter was very, very supportive outwardly, and then she's a sweet person and she's a girl. She was very supportive. Tupac was supportive, too. They both were. After I had been there for about ninety days, Tupac wrote me a letter this thick and told me how he had felt, and that he couldn't be that excited because he didn't know whether this was real or not, though he hoped it was. How I hurt him, and abandoned them, and it was not a hate letter. It was a loving, honest, truthful letter, but I was devastated."

"Do you still have it?" I ask her.

"What?" She says.

"Tupac's letter."

"I think so." Afeni gets up and goes to the back corner of her bedroom. I hope she has the letter. So much of her material memories are long gone from all her moving around —pictures, poems, journals—so now she stores her memories in her head. In fact, other people have more pictures of Afeni than she has of herself.

Tupac must have known his mother travels light because he gave his own writings and poems to Leila Steinberg for safekeeping. And it's a good thing. Because what Afeni has long lost in time, Tupac had recorded in prose. This poem is from *The Rose that Grew from Concrete,* a collection of Tupac's poetry.

When Ure Hero Falls
(My Hero My Mother)

When your hero falls from grace
all fairy tales R uncovered
myths exposed and pain magnified
The greatest pain discovered
U taught me 2 be strong
But I'm confused 2 C U so weak
U said never 2 give up
and it hurts 2 C U welcome defeat
When ure Hero falls so do the stars
and so does the perception of tomorrow
without my Hero there is only
me alone 2 deal with my sorrow.
Your heart ceases 2 work
and your soul is not happy at all.
What R U expected 2 do
when ure only Hero falls

I'm sure the letter she received from him in rehab was reflective of this poem.

"I can't find the letter." Afeni returns from her closet. "But I remember how it affected me. I went to my sponsor with the letter because I was so messed up over it. That's when she taught me humility. I was so devastated, and she helped me. She helped me because she told me that the only reason that I was devastated was because my pride was hurt. This is what she would do. She made me see when it was my pride getting in the way of doing the right thing. It was very hard, but she did that for me. I remember I was seeing this guy, Franklin, in the program."

"Afeni, you're not supposed to do that!" I laugh.

"Child, I know." She shakes her head. "So listen to what happened. I found out that he was fuckin' somebody that I was sponsoring. He had sex with somebody or tried to have sex, but she wouldn't. She came back and told me. I went to my sponsor and you know what she told me? 'Are you married to him?' I said no. She said, 'Then it's none of your business who is having sex with him.'"

"Damn," I say. "She's cold."

"She was right. But, of course, I didn't get that at the time. I looked at her like she was nuts. This bitch is out of her fucking mind. What the fuck is she talking about, you know. But she was right, and the thing is, that woman never lied to me. She loved me. As a human being coming off of drugs, she had love for me, and real concern.

"So I couldn't ever dismiss what she said even though I wanted to so bad. That's the kind of shit that she would do for me, and that was good because when I left there and ended up having to deal with my son and my daughter about my life, what happened? I had to listen to my children tell me what *they* had experienced. And I couldn't say nothing. I had to listen, and I did. I had been taught my place. That woman taught me my place really well. If she hadn't done that I would not have been able to face my children and hear their pain."

How does a mother reconcile within herself having caused that much pain for their child?

"Do you forgive yourself, Afeni?" I wonder if she will always be guilt-ridden. She thinks a minute before she answers me. I know it won't be a simple yes or no response.

"I feel sorry for people who are not addicts or alcoholics because doing those steps changed my life. I learned lessons about how to live from that program." Afeni reaches for the blue AA book that is always nearby. She reads for a minute and forgets I'm there. She turns the book over on her lap and removes her glasses. She leans into me and says, "One of the things I had to admit was that I had murdered a child in my stomach. I had caused the death of a baby. I couldn't hide behind an abortion or my right to choose or anything. I know very well that I went into an abortion clinic, and I caused them to put a needle into my navel and stop the heartbeat of a living human being. I had to ask God to please forgive me for that. That was the worst thing that I had done. And the rest of it, I had to rely on, have faith, in this program." She places her hand tenderly over the little blue paperback. "This is a program of faith. I had to have faith that if I asked God with a sincere heart, and if I asked that child that was in my belly, I would be forgiven.

"When I finished the fifth step, my sponsor took that paper that I had written all that stuff on and burned it, so I could release that pain. It's not that I didn't do those things, but I don't have to walk away with that from there,

with that weight on me. I still practice this. In order to st
healthy and clean, I confess before God *and* a witness. First
another human being should bear witness to the fact that
you did this because addicts are tricky, and we could fool
ourselves into believing something really didn't occur. On
top of that I must ask for forgiveness. Having done that, I
have to have faith that I have done what I could and it is
time to learn from my errors."

"Why is it so important to tell someone? Why in a
group with a bunch of strangers? That seems so unnatural,
like undressing in public or doing a love scene—which I
hate doing." I cringe at the thought of such intimate exposure. "Is this to humiliate you?"

"Because you have to get out of yourself. You have to
learn that your shit stinks like everybody else's. Sharing
with other people helps you get out of your own head. Listening to other people share is the only way you hear the
message sometimes. The Blue Book gives you thinking and
living skills. You have to be willing to do each step. The next
step is when you are entirely ready to have God remove
these character defects, inside of yourself. You have to have
a desire to have this poison removed from you any way that
God chooses to do it. The most important thing is to do it.
Then we ask him to remove our shortcomings, and that's it.
Then you make a list of all the persons you've harmed.

"You need to become willing to make amends to them.
Amends is not just saying I'm sorry. You have to admit
what you've done and acknowledge it. The people that I

harmed, I had to go to all those people and make amends. So I made a list."

"Ugh," I groan, "this shit just gets worse and worse. Don't they know you're sorry? Don't they already know that you feel bad and you're getting help and trying to fix yourself?"

"This is not just I'm sorry, kiss and make up, Jasmine. This is about *them*, my children, my sister, my family, and hearing *them* and taking responsibility for what I did to *them*. When I go to make amends, I have no control. I'm not *in charge*," she says disdainfully. I made an appointment with each person and told them I had something to talk to them about. I told them they didn't have to meet with me. They didn't have to do anything. They may be so pissed or hurt that they were through with me and maybe they didn't want to hear my shit. And I had to deal with that—I can't force anyone. I can't do anything, except pray that they will see me. One-on-one. No interruptions. I was required to admit what I did wrong to that person. I could not justify my wrongdoings. I could not explain it. You have to listen to their response."

"How did they all respond?" I can only imagine Tupac's reaction after having read his poems. I know how deeply hurt he was by Afeni's drug addiction.

"My sister just gave me a hug and my daughter also. But my son had lots of questions. He wanted to go over a few things." She smiles, remembering Tupac and his questions. Afeni, in her turn, would probably have nailed *her* mama the same way had the tables been turned. "You know what? The amends to my son weren't the hardest. The hardest was really to my daughter. That's the hardest amends that I had to make. Because I abandoned Sekyiwa emotionally, in puberty. I'm a woman; I know all the shit that she went through. She ended up getting pregnant. She was a good girl, and I changed her whole path. My behavior changed her whole personality." Tears flow so immediately with this admission. I wonder how they got here so fast. "I take responsibility for that. I ain't fuckin' around with that. They got rights, my kids. I did some damage, but I don't live in the damage. I've made the amends. My sponsor told me to try the best amend I could make—a living amends, by living a life that doesn't have those things in it. That's what I really try to do. That's the only thing my family would believe—what *they* see.

"The best thing about when Tupac died is that he had five and a half years of his mother being healthy. . . . Healthier than I was before I was using, and we had a much healthier relationship."

"When Tupac was laid up in New York, it seemed like to me that he was still making you pay," I tell Afeni. He liked having Afeni do for him, cook for him, and wait on him. It was like he was saying, "Be my mommy."

"He always made me pay. He had a right. . . . I don't have a right. I don't care. It doesn't matter. I don't get to have that. I gave that up. I accept that. That's how I work on my pride and humility. That ain't nothing, you know what I mean. That's *my* weight and I have to carry my weight. The only issue is how I carry it and how I do it. If I'm really recovered, then I won't be defeated by it . . . and keep moving toward a better life. I try to be there for other people. I try to help instead of tear down. I know mistakes are possible but dignity is possible after those mistakes."

It's so dark on the porch, I can only see Afeni's face by the glow of her cigarette.

"If I hadn't used crack, I would probably still be using drugs. Because what crack does is it eliminates your ability to be social. Crack is all about crack. Nothing else . . . You just gotta get more crack. Crack is about you smoke, and you need to smoke some more. It never ends. You need to always have more. That's all it's about."

"That's why they call them crack *fiends*." I say. "Do you remember losing your grip on yourself or do you just remember realizing you had no grip?"

"I remember realizing that I had no grip. That's what Tupac didn't forgive me for for the longest time. Because Tupac asked me if I was using drugs and I told him I was smoking, but I had it under control. I told them that there was no problem. And my son believed me. And that's why he didn't forgive me, because I lied. Basically that's what it was for him. He never got past that I lied about having it under control. It didn't even get to nothing else but that."

"And he's not used to you lying." One thing the Shakurs need as a family is the truth. The three of them—Afeni and her kids—are profoundly betrayed by lies.

"That's what I mean. Lying was not our reality," Afeni

agrees. "So much so that that lie is what ultimately did it for him. He couldn't get over it."

"But didn't you *think* you had it under control? I mean is it really lying if you think you're telling the truth?"

Afeni is quiet again. She answers me slowly, like I'm too young to fully understand. "Addicts lie. That's what they do. They keep secrets and they lie. That's why I don't even play with some shit. I don't keep secrets 'cause I can't afford them. Somebody's got to know what's going on with me at all times.

"Quite frankly, we all think that our worst things are the most horrible. We all have them, and knowing that frees me from keeping secrets and getting sick again. The ugliest thing, the worst feeling, I have to share it with somebody and I don't lie."

Afeni begins, but I look out into the black night. Even the floodlights illuminating the wooded pines seem to fade.

"When I lost my son, I had to remember I had a daughter and I had grandchildren and I have a responsibility to my son to stay clean and live up to my duties. And my duties did not end when Tupac died." She looks at me and drags on her Newport. A smile creeps across her eyes as she pulls on the menthol. "You and Jada helped me see that. I'll never forget that conversation. . . ."

I remember the conversation. I remember that, and it was a painful day. It was a Sunday, two days after Tupac died. He died Friday, September 13. Afeni had him cremated that Saturday morning and returned to Los Angeles with his ashes that night. I was with the family when Afeni got there. They all looked like zombies and I occupied Afeni's little niece, Imani, while they cried.

Jada Pinkett Smith, Tupac's old and trusted friend, met me Sunday morning at my house. Our mission was to go to get Afeni, pick her up from the Westwood condominium, take her away from the family, and warn her of what lay ahead. I remember the conversation:

"The vultures are coming to get you, Afeni." I look into her puffy eyes as if she could really hear us.

"You need to get in there. Find out what Pac owned, what Pac had. You need some lawyers." Jada laid it out.

"You need accountants," I said firmly.

"And we can help you. We can help you with all of that," Jada reassures. "But you got to be ready. 'Cause this ain't no joke. We all know how Pac kept his business, his money, his agreements."

"You need to understand everything Tupac owned, everything he created," I said to Afeni. "They are going to come after you like you're the poor little widow lady."

"They don't know shit," Jada confronts Afeni. "You don't know about his production company. You don't know about his finances. You don't know about Death Row or Suge Knight or what kind of agreements he had on the table."

Afeni was stunned and broken like a one-winged bird. We held her close that day and cried. We prayed for her and asked God to give her the strength to stand up for Tupac.

Now, as Afeni remembers that conversation, I wonder

why she smiles at such a painful day when I can remember how much she hurt.

"If you and Jada hadn't done that on that day, that would have been it," she says with pride. "And do you know I *heard* you. If you had not been that hard on me on *that* day, it would have been gone. *All* of it would have been gone."

Little did I know at that moment, September 15, 1996, that Afeni would spend the next seven years fighting to keep Tupac's works alive and in the family.

NINE

Rise

"Out of the huts of history's shame, I rise.
Up from the past that's rooted in pain, I rise."
—MAYA ANGELOU

The first in line to siphon Tupac's money was Billy Garland, also known as "the sperm donor"—the father Tupac had never known. Tupac was twenty-three years old and was already famous when he met Billy for the first time, in 1994; he was lying critically wounded when Billy showed up at his bedside. Tupac talked to him a little bit, and during the encounter Afeni sat quietly in a corner on the carpet giving space to her bed-ridden son, at the same time letting Billy know he did not have the full floor. Oh, yes, and Billy showed up again in 1996 at the Las Vegas hospital where Tupac lay in a coma.

I wonder what good it does for the dying when you're there for them at the end of their lives, but you never showed up for them while they were living. As far as Billy Garland goes, he seemed to have popped up out of nowhere, at least from where I sat. I knew of the men who had raised Tupac, who had loved Tupac. I had heard all the stories about Tupac's uncle Tom and his stepfather Mutulu, but I had never heard the name Billy Garland mentioned. I had heard all the "when-Tupac-was-a-baby" stories, and Billy Garland's name had never come up. Legs was mentioned, this tough, colorful street dude who respected Afeni and loved her little boy. Took him to the barber-shop and McDonald's and called him his son. I had heard about Legs, but not Billy Garland. It was Crooksie who painted Afeni and Tupac's first bedroom when Afeni moved in with Glo. And there was Tupac's godfather, Cochise, who wrote him loving and careful letters from prison all through Tupac's growing up. I had heard how Glo kissed the newborn Tupac from head to toe as soon as he came out of the womb. But I had never heard stories of Billy Garland.

So, when I heard the news that Billy Garland was making claim to Tupac's money, I wondered how this man could stand in a courtroom in front of strangers and say he was this boy's *father*. I wondered, as I heard of this absurd lawsuit, how he could hold his head high enough to even *see* his way into a courtroom after not living one moment in the child's life. I wondered how he could take the tears of a grieving mother, as tough as that mother may be, and flaunt those tears in front of a judge and lawyers and say "I want some of what's left for *her* for myself." It's incredible that a person who has never provided anything for a child as that child grows up would try to take what that child has made for himself on his own. All Billy Garland ever did for Tupac was create a void, which Tupac in all futility searched to fill for most of his life.

So one of Afeni's first trials after Tupac died was to go up against Billy Garland. Fortunately, she was ready. By now, having been warned by Jada and me, she had a "team." She had lawyers, Donald David and Rick Fischbein. She had an accountant, Jeffrey Joiner, who began sifting and sorting through Tupac's layers of financial madness. And she had Deloitte and Touche, the firm that audited Interscope Records and located Tupac's outstanding compensation.

But as soon as one case was closed another one started. Before long Afeni was in court, sometimes in concurrent cases, for years. Yet with each moment of adversity, she came out the wiser and the stronger.

Over the years, I have left messages for Afeni, basically checking in to see if she's all right; she has left messages in return. Once, she called me before I went to D.C. to star in the musical *Chicago*. "You go on and do what you're supposed to do," she told me. "I see you up there in *Chicago*! That's what you're supposed to do. You wear that shit out, Jasmine. Don't worry about me. I'm good. I'm good *now* because I say to myself 'there's a beginning, a middle, and an end to everything.' Right now I'm just in the middle, but I know there will be an end."

Over the years I have gone months without reaching her. My only contact would be through secondhand updates from various assistants and family members. One time an assistant calls me. "Afeni is in L.A. for two days," she says. "One day is booked with meetings and the other day in court. But she really wants to see you. Meet us at the Beverly Hills Hotel at two-thiry. She has an hour before she leaves for the airport."

I get there on time, and Afeni is so happy to see me. "I wanted you to see my house," I say to Afeni, disappointed she cannot stop by.

"Fuck the house, I need to see that baby. How is she?" Afeni smiles.

"Running things," I answer, referring to my three-year-old.

"Yep, that's what she's here to do," she chuckles, "but you know I can't stay here long. I gotta get out of L.A. It's been two days too long."

Afeni hates L.A., and has never been back to Vegas since Tupac died. She only spends time in *northern* California, where the coastal beauty of San Francisco, Sausalito, and Oakland soothe her mind. Those cities bear no sickening memories for Afeni. Those cities smell of crisp, clean, blue calm, not the thick smoggy red of grief.

"So, what's going on now?" I ask, knowing if it isn't Interscope, it's Death Row she's either meeting or fighting.

I'm not sure who's meeting Afeni at Spago's, and who's meeting her at the courthouse.

I look around the hotel suite for a chair. There are people in the room, and I know them all. There's Tupac's high-school friend, Molly, who is Afeni's assistant, and a couple of guys for security. Afeni sits on her bed with an ashtray. She is pleased, almost bubbly. She wants to talk, which means she had a good day.

"I don't know what you know about the documentary film," she begins. "But we had meetings today with MTV and Paramount, and can I just thank you for Karolyn Ali?" Afeni looks at me still beaming but serious. Karolyn Ali is a producer friend of mine that I met on the movie *Kla$h* in 1994. We stayed in touch and I brought her to Atlanta to coordinate Tupac's memorial, which had become a huge production. Her ease and skills proved invaluable to the Shakur family at that time, and she was an excellent first choice to run the film and book division of Afeni's new company, Amaru Entertainment, Inc.

"You're welcome," I say to Afeni. "She's a beautiful person."

"Fuck that," Afeni says, lighting a Newport. "She's a grown-ass woman, and it's a helluva thing to have a grown woman on the team."

Afeni's a grown-ass woman, too, but I know what she means. Karolyn is confident, articulate, worldly. She knows how to negotiate; she knows how to pitch. She knows how to talk on the phone. She knows how to conduct business without carrying the weight of her personal problems into the office. She knows how to talk to all kinds of people— white men, Black women, young brothers or sassy sisters, family members, business associates, money folk or moody artists—and just in case, should the need ever arise, she can be a bitch if she has to.

"I'm so proud. We are partners." Afeni goes on. "On this MTV project they get real humbled by us because they always start out thinking we don't know what we're talking about, but we *do*! They start out thinking we're arrogant and we're *not*! We just do our work. We stay focused and do what we say were going to do. And I'm so proud of that." Afeni's on a roll. "We never argue with them. We just fucking work. Because we are such good, efficient workers we always catch them at the end and show them a piece of paper. I'm so proud of my team. And at the end of the day, I did my job. It's over. After that God has it and the people have it."

Afeni's exuberant revelation echoes her Panther years. For the first time since I've known her, I see who that young Afeni was. I see the power of her conviction in its fullest articulation. I see Afeni find her purpose again—this time without anger, this time with humility, this time connected to God. This time, she thinks before she acts. This time she is clear about what is right and what is wrong, about what is her responsibility and what is out of her control. Afeni is passionate again. She is high today, but not on crack cocaine.

One of the big guys passes a fruit platter my way. I grab

some pineapple chunks and a mango slice. "What piece of paper are you talking about?" I'm trying to catch up on all that has transpired at Amaru. I see they've been busy. "What do you mean you always catch them at the end and show them a piece of paper?"

"Contracts, Jasmine. I've become a firm believer in contracts."

"What?" I say. "Are you kidding me?" I'm shocked. Is this the same woman who I dragged kicking and screaming to my lawyer's office in 1995 so we could have a legal and documented agreement about my producing her life story? Is this the same woman who sucked her teeth every time the great burden of signing her name arose? Is this the same woman I insisted accept checks from my production company to option the rights of her story? "Ain't nobody doing my story but you," she used to tell me. "I don't need some paper. I don't want your money either."

"Afeni, this is how it's done," I had explained to her. "This is how you protect yourself. I have a certain amount of time to get this project done, then you can take it somewhere else." She didn't want to hear it then. Tupac was still alive and definitely running things, so she couldn't be bothered with paper and contracts. She knew she'd never screw me, so what was the point? She'd never leave us behind—me or my sister Monica, who interviewed Afeni extensively and wrote the treatment for our movie about her. Afeni would never leave us behind, so why did she need a contract? Now I listen to her espouse the virtues of having a contract and I can't believe how savvy she's become.

"We went back and wrote every contract that Tupac hadn't done," she tells me. "He had *no* contracts with producers, which meant all of *their* money was still at Interscope, waiting to be claimed!"

"Collecting interest," I add.

"Yes, being used by the record company. They knew these artists would never claim it, because there was no paperwork, no contracts. If it hadn't been for Amaru, and this child right here," she points to Molly, who turns a little pink, "no one would have gotten paid. Molly remembers everything. She knows who produced what song. Who sang on it. Who was in the studio bullshitting when they recorded it and who was really contributing; she remembers all that shit. And these people, these musicians and singers, would not have asked Tupac for a fucking dime. They wouldn't have and they didn't. Because they loved Tupac. They just wanted to work with him. The record company knew that and they took advantage of that. What they do on every album is just take money out of the artist's account. They take money and put it over to the side." She makes an imaginary pile of money with her hands and slides it to the side of the bed. "I made it possible for those people in the music industry to get paid. We aren't going down like that."

"That's the old Motown way," I say with a smile.

"I know we aren't doing that to those people. I'm proud of that, too. We got those artists paid." Afeni flips an orange slice inside out and pulls the juicy meat off the peel with her teeth. But then Molly points to her watch. It's time to go.

I don't get Afeni all to myself anymore, not for hours at a time, but I get what I can. I'd rather see her for half an hour living in glory than for sixteen hours of pain. Life does turn around if you can just wait it out.

As Molly packs up Afeni's toiletries in the bathroom, the big guys call for a bellman. Afeni looks at me with tears in her eyes and says, "And we pay our taxes, Jasmine. I don't owe six million dollars in taxes for 1997, not for 1998, 1999, 2000, 2001 or 2002, and neither does my son. Okay? So I have these quiet victories. I don't owe nothing! Can you imagine that?" She rises from the bed and hugs me again. "I cannot thank you enough," she says in my ear. "And God bless Jeff Joiner." Her accountant and my brother-in-law.

They are packed up and gone within minutes, and I'm left in a room I didn't check in to. I sit on the bed among newspaper pages and digest Afeni's new stories. Her enthusiasm lingers in the room like firefly glow. She was so happy today, so grateful to be thriving. She faces the monster music industry each day with nothing but a slingshot, and she emerges triumphant. She's finishing Tupac's projects for him. She runs his company, produces his films, releases his music, and publishes his books. She runs the performing arts center erected in his name as he had instructed her. "She is a CEO," I say to myself.

The bed is a mess. It holds the only clues that Afeni was once here. I carry the ashtray to the bathroom and dump the butts into the toilet. I toss her empty Evian bottles into a nearby wastebasket. As I start to gather the newspaper pages strewn in a loose arc around the edges of the bed-spread, I notice an article from today's *Los Angeles Times*. It is folded neatly and creased as if someone had just finished reading it. July 13, 2002, page B-3, by *Times* staff writer Jennifer Sinco Kelleher. The first line reads:

> Rap mogul Marian "Suge" Knight received notice this week from the Internal Revenue Service, claiming he owes about $6 million in personal income taxes, his attorney said Friday.

Ahh, that's where Afeni got that six-million dollar figure from. I had wondered why Afeni so specifically said that Tupac didn't owe *six million* in taxes.

> The IRS notice adds to the financial turmoil surrounding the owner of music label The Row Records, formerly known as Death Row Records.
>
> It comes just months after Knight's former lawyer, David Kenner, was sentenced to three years' probation in April after he admitted to hiding more than $4 million in earnings from the IRS.

Well, Afeni should be proud of her small victories. So many artists lose their entire estate when they die, and so many go bankrupt. So many folk don't pay their taxes and lose everything to the IRS. Good job, Afeni. For someone who never had money or cared about music, you had quite a lesson in capitalism and paying your way.

The next time I'm in Atlanta, I keep my promise to Afeni and take my daughter to see her. She greets us on her front porch and reaches for me. I pass the American flag hanging from one of the wooden posts and take note. It's been there since 9/11, so it's not my first time seeing it. An American flag always catches my eye, but the irony of one hanging from the Shakur front porch is especially arresting. The idea that this woman once labeled an enemy of the state, once accused of conspiracy to bomb Abercrombie and Fitch, now exposes her patriotic solidarity, so publicly reveals the danger of reducing complex personalities to a single label. People are layered. Before I knew the real reason for her to hang the American flag, I had my *own* theory.

I think the flag for Afeni represents *the people*, not necessarily *the government*, and that *the people* for Afeni now went beyond the disenfranchised of Harlem and the Bronx. The people are those attacked. The people are those dead and gone. Afeni is always down with the underdog. And today, the underdog is the victim of 9/11. She is not down with the terrorist murderers of Al Qaeda. She sympathizes with the people of America.

My theory, I discover, is a bit esoteric in comparison to Afeni's *real* reason for displaying the flag. Deeply moved by the loss of life in the World Trade Center attack, she told me this story: "Deloitte and Touche, our auditors, were located in the World Trade Center on September 11 when the towers came down, and they had to leave the building. They panicked, ran out of their offices. And then they remembered they had left Tupac's stuff on the desk. . . . Jasmine, they went back and got his shit. Yes they did. Got his shit off the fuckin' desk." Afeni slapped her thigh. "Then they left that building. God is such a good God. He works in all these ways and places. Can you imagine that?" She looked at me. "I thought about it. I thought about what they did, and I said I would never have done that. I was real humbled by that. They ran back and got all of Tupac's shit."

Now as I pass Afeni's American flag, I think of those people in that office that ran back to get Tupac's papers. Every account of money going in and money going out, every last bit of proof of that man's work, they went back and got it. Their lives were spared, too. I think of them as I pass Afeni's flag for a moment. That is why it is hanging, so we don't forget.

Imani, my daughter, acts shy at first but Afeni leaves her alone. She speaks to her like she speaks to me. No baby talk or condescension. Eventually Imani comes around. She hugs Afeni, asks her for some water, and while we're in the kitchen Imani wonders if Afeni has cheese toast. We make her some. Then we sit down in the kitchen while she eats it.

"That right there," she nods towards Imani. "Her job is to anchor you. She anchors her mother. She makes you know your place in the universe. That ain't no easy job, but they do that. That's what your children do. That's what mine did for me."

I know Imani's listening intently but I don't think she knows what *anchor* means. "Without them? Oh please," Afeni thinks for a moment. "What I would have gone and done? Kids boomerang you back to sanity. My daughter kept me from going crazy." Imani devours the center of the bread, leaving the crust on her plate.

"When my son was . . ." Afeni doesn't say the word killed. "I never forgot I had another child standing there hurting just as bad as I was. I knew she needed me. I knew my first job was to my daughter. She was the living. I could not just check out 'cause he wasn't here anymore."

"Can I have more water?" Imani asks.

"What do you say?" I prod.

"Please," Imani adds.

Afeni's already up and getting it.

"My mommy has a baby brother in her tummy." Imani blurts out, sure to catch Afeni's attention.

Afeni looks to me in surprise, and I shake my head no. "She just knows I want one." I smile at Imani, who smirks at me like she knows something I don't.

"It'll be here," Afeni says returning with the water, "as soon as the one God has for you moves to the front of the line. You know, you don't choose children, children choose you. That baby will be here exactly when that baby should be here. Ask once and leave it alone. Never beg."

"But Imani's four. I didn't want them to be too far apart," I protest, like there's anything I plan to do about it. Or is there?

"Ask once," she reiterates. "Don't—"

At that moment the front door bursts open and three big-eyed children rush into the kitchen. Nzingha and Malik, Afeni's grandchildren and another Imani, Jamala's daughter, Afeni's grandniece.

I met Afeni's Imani when she was only two, now she's ten. My little Imani meets their bigger Imani for the first time. Big Imani smiles down on my little one. "I'm Imani, too," she says proudly. My Imani appears skeptical. "For real," I say to her. "Her name is also Imani." My little one says, "Oh," not so sure she likes sharing the name. The kids snatch her up and take her downstairs to all their toys. The house feels light, buoyant with the aroma of toasted bread in the air.

"Wow," I say to Afeni, "this goes by fast. It's like warp speed after you turn thirty, huh?" She laughs. "Thirteen to twenty-two took forever," I add.

"It's all about acceptance. Accepting time. Accepting change. And change was a big one for me to accept because

I could always feel it coming." She is thoughtful now, but not sad. "The winds of change. I could always feel them," she says again. "Before the change occurs even. I used to *react* to the winds because I would be thrown off by them. I felt out of control, and I didn't like that. Now I know that when change is coming I must be calm. I must be still instead of frantic. I visualize that tennis player in the backcourt." She plants down that foot and sways back and forth. She sways but she is grounded. "This is my evolutionary understanding of the matter. We flow through these winds of danger, distress, and confusion to be able to be sure-footed on the other side. What we must do now is do these things that we are duty bound to do. Have you read *Shogun*?" She looks at me directly. She's asked me this before.

"Well, *Shogun* teaches the purist principle of martial arts—duty and honor. Accepting your duty and finding honor in doing it." She reminds me again.

"Duty bound." Afeni rises. "Let's go to the back to my room." I figure she needs a smoke by now.

"I have to go soon. Daddy's making dinner," I say walking down the hallway to her room.

Afeni walks straight through her bedroom and out to the back porch and stops short of the screened railing. CNN flickers in the corner on mute, and we can hear the kids laughing from the basement beneath us. I grab her pack of Newports and lighter from her lawn chair and join her at the railing.

"Thank you, baby," she says lighting up. "I know you have to go, I just needed to see your child."

"I know, that's why I brought her by."

"And I needed to see you," she adds.

That makes me want to cry, although I'm not sure why. I feel tight in my throat so I don't respond. I just let Afeni do the talking, which was easy to do since she had something to say. I'm used to crying with Afeni. We've been through a lot of life together. So I don't know why I can't cry now. I guess I don't want to. I want to be happy right now and enjoy the kids, the pine trees, and the smell of toast. Sometimes I feel like I hold her heart in my hands, and I must be very careful. I know Afeni's pain, but I know her joy, too.

"I rely heavily also on my belief in the sacrifice of Christ. The utter beauty of his sacrifice, the grace that flows from that. I think if it hadn't been for that one act, I don't know where human beings would be. Thank God he did that one act. I believe it made it possible for us to be forgiven without having to do anything to have redemption except to say, 'God, can you help me?' How easy it is to get God's attention. To me, that's the most beautiful of them all. . . . The redemption of that innocent blood that fell on that cross. For me, with all the shit that I've done in my life, it's the grace of God that took the desire for cocaine out of me. I got myself into crack, but it was God who brought me out. God couldn't get my attention until he gave me that crack pipe. The only way my stupid, stubborn brain would get it. And these are not *new* lessons. Other people been knowing this shit. But I had to be brought to my knees."

There is a long moment before I speak as I wait for the swell in my throat to go down. "I hear you, Afeni," I finally say. And I did hear her. As I hear my nana, my mother, my father. As I hear all the great teachers in my life that have pulled me aside and out of earshot of classmates of fellow dancers to tell me something I needed to hear.

I hear you Afeni, like I hear my mother say *Embrace your beauty.* Like I hear my father say *You are more than a performer, Jasmine. You are a full human being.* As I hear Geoffrey Holder, director of *The Wiz,* say *Don't let any man take your spirit.* Kelvin Rotardier, director of the Alvin Ailey Workshop Company, say *Be consistent.* Mary Barnett say *Lift your eyes. . . .*

I hear you, Afeni, say *Live life from here. Pick up from where I am now. I give my experience to you so you don't have to go down like I did to learn it.*

"I know you hear me, Jasmine," Afeni assures me. "I just had to say it. I can't keep nothing heavy on my heart."

I gather my child and walk the long drive to my car. The grandbabies scream good-byes from the front porch and wave with passion.

"Oh, don't forget." Afeni runs behind me to the car. "Sweet Honey in the Rock at the Wilshire Ebell on December seventh. Call Dina [Afeni's music lawyer]. She's getting the tickets, and we're all going. You must come, Jasmine.

Sweet Honey in the Rock." She hugs me and looks me in the eye. "You must come."

On that crisp December night I felt so appreciative, so glad she invited me particularly to this concert, on this night... with her. The five women of Sweet Honey in the Rock were alive like fire. Blue. Red. Orange. Yellow. An explosion of beauty and soul.

Each woman is so different. Ysaye Maria Barnwell has deep-chocolate, smooth, glowing skin with smiling eyes. She stands strong and grounded with high breasts and cheekbones reaching past her height. She sings low, lower than I've heard any woman ever sing. Her voice is round and rhythmic as she holds the bottom. Aisha Kahlil is like a bird, a long-legged, far-reaching ibis. She dances as she sings as if her body cannot speak from only one language. Her sister, Nitanju Bolade Casel, equals her stature. Like runway models they are stunning and thin, but their power transcends the Atlantic. At times they seem to call back to Africa, and at other moments they seem to sing to us *from* the Motherland instead of America. Sometimes it is hard to know which coast of the Atlantic these sisters sing from. Carol Maillard, the fourth woman, is warm and funky. Her golden caramel skin radiates joy, fun joy, like someone on the verge of a party. Her face is bright, her features big, round, and expressive. I hear her sultry alto through the pulse of the background rhythms. I recognize her voice because I worked with Carol years ago in a show called *Bee-hive* at the Village Gate in New York. I played with her baby, Jordan, in the dressing rooms of the Gate's cellar. Now, Jordan is a man.

Bernice Johnson Reagon steps forward from the group and speaks to the audience. She is smart and political, funny and wise. She is the founder of Sweet Honey in the Rock and keeper of the voice. Of this beautiful group of women she says: "I walk Sweet Honey in the Rock as a path, a discipline. I do not create the path which has been carried out by the living and dying of those who walked it before me with their lives, but I make my own tracks on this mountainous road. Sweet Honey is that way, it is that path."

Bernice Johnson Reagon steps back a few steps to rejoin the arc of the other four women. As she starts to sing, a deep, brown, willful tone reaches us from her gut. I have a revelation. This voice, the voice of Bernice Johnson Reagon, is Afeni's voice. If Afeni could sing she would sing in the voice of Bernice Johnson Reagon. I know because Afeni sits to my left tonight, and I feel everything change when Reagon begins to sing. Afeni calls up her own voice and sings right along with Bernice Johnson Reagon. Their voices lock like praying hands desperate to find God. Afeni knows every word, every inflection Bernice Johnson Reagon delivers.

We who believe in freedom cannot rest.
We who believe in freedom cannot rest until it comes.

In my ear to my left I hear Afeni sing. She raises her hands towards Sweet Honey and sings through her pain and her triumphs. She sings through the death of her son.

> *Until the killing of Black men, Black mother's son*
> *is as important as the killing of White men, White mother's*
>   *son*
> *we who believe in freedom cannot rest.*

She sings through her Panther years.

> *That what touches me most*
> *is that I had a chance to work with people.*
> *Passing on to others,*
> *that which was passed on to me.*

Through the healing of her daughter's spirit.

> *To me young people come first;*
> *they have the courage where we fail.*

Through realizing the dream of the Tupac Amaru Shakur Performing Arts Center where little children, like young Tupac, can go for artistic nourishment;

> *is when the reins are in the hand of the young,*
> *who dare to run against the storm.*
> *We who believe . . .*

The chorus swells and I close my eyes. I fill up with this call to freedom. I fill up until I feel the water rise in my eyes. I have come to a sacred place tonight with Sweet Honey in the Rock. I have been here before in church listening to my father, in theatres watching Alvin Ailey, in arenas with Anita Baker. I am grateful I am here now.

Afeni's is the only voice I hear for a moment singing in my left ear. She possesses the next verse as if it were written just for her. It is her testimony.

> *I'm a woman who speaks in a voice*
> *and I must be heard*
> *at times I can be quite difficult,*
> *I'll bow to no man's word.*

This *is* Afeni. This song is written for her. As Afeni's story is written for me. At this moment I am so grateful she has let me know her. I reach for her hand, as she sings away. I grab it to say *thank you*. Thank you for trusting me. Thank you for falling in front of me and for getting back up. Thank you for believing in me what I could not see for myself. Thank you for inviting me here tonight. She squeezes my hand back without looking my way and never drops a note of the song. . . . *You're welcome.*

Bibliography

Angelou, Maya. *Still I Rise*. New York: Random House, 2001.

Anonymous, Alcoholics. *Alcoholics Anonymous*. Croton Falls: New York: The Anonymous Press, 1996.

——. *Twelve Steps and Twelve Traditions*. New York: Alcoholics Anonymous World Services, Inc., 1953

Archer, Jules. *They Had A Dream, The Civil Rights Struggle from Frederick Douglass to Marcuss Garvey to Martin Luther King Jr. and Malcom X*. New York: Puffin Books,1996.

Brown, Claude. *Manchild In The Promised Land*. New York: Signet, 1965.

Boyd, Herb. *Black Panthers for Beginners*. Writers and Readers Publishing, 1995.

Look for Me in the Whirlwind: The Collective Autobiography of the New York 21. Foreword by Hayward Burns. New York: Vintage Books, 1971.

Carroll, Rebecca. *I Know What the Red Clay Looks Like*. New York: Crown, 1994.

Cleage, Pearl. *Deals With the Devil*. New York: Ballantine, 1987.

Cleaver, Eldridge. *Soul On Ice*. New York: Dell Publishing Co., Inc., 1968.

Cronon, E. David. *Black Moses: The Story of Marcus Garvey and the Universal Negro Improvement Association*. Madison: The University of Wisconsin Press, 1969.

Davis, Angela. *Angela Davis: An Autobiography*. New York: International Publishers, 1988.

Dial, Adolph L., Eliades, David K. *The Only Land I Know*. New York: Syracuse University Press, 1996.

Dyson, Michael Eric. *Holler If You Hear Me*. New York: Basic Civitas Books, 2001.

Gitlin, Todd. *The Sixties: Years of Hope, Days of Rage*. New York: Bantam Books, 1987.

Gonzalez-Wippler, Migene. *Legends of Santeria*. St. Paul: Llewellyn Publications, 1994.

——. *Santeria The Religion*. St. Paul: Llewellyn Publications, 1994.

hooks, bell. *Black Looks: race and representation*. Boston: South End Press, 1992.

hooks, bell. *Sisters of the Yam: Black Women and Self-recovery*. Boston: South End Press, 1986.

Lawler, Mary. *Marcus Garvey, Black Nationalist Leader*. Los Angeles: Melrose Square Publishing Company, 1988.

Lemann, Nicholas. *The Promised Land: The Great Black Migration and How It Changed America*. New York: Vintage Books, 1996.

My Soul Looks Back, 'Less I Forget, A Collection of Quotations By People of Color. Edited by Dorothy Winbush Riley. New York: Harper Collins Publishers, Inc., 1993. "Dark Days," *City Arts Quarterly*, spring 1988.

Randall, Dudley. *The Black Poets*. New York: Bantam Books, 1985.

Shakur, Tupac Amaru. *The Rose that Grew from Concrete*. New York: MTV Books/Pocket Books, 1999.

Woititz, Janet Geringer. *Adult Children of Alcoholics*. Deerfield Beach: Health Communications, Inc., 1993.

Index

farm of, 9–10
as fighter, 32–34, 47, 57, 61–62,
   64, 66, 72, 95–96, 99, 121
as friend, 4, 150, 204
on God's grace, 171, 173, 181,
   182, 200, 204–5
Guy's first meeting of (at
   Tupac's hearing), 3–4
Guy's visits with, 5–7, 27–30
on helping others, 62, 63–64,
   126, 185, 199
house of, 6–7, 8–9
in L.A., 192–99
land valued by, 7–8, 9–10
Legal Services work of, 126, 127,
   141
letter to her children from,
   86–88
life story as movie or book, 2,
   49–51, 55, 59, 95–96, 113–16,
   132, 136, 137, 144, 145–46,
   152–53, 161–62, 195
loss of son, 54–55, 187–88, 201;
   see also Shakur, Tupac
loss of spirit, 165–67
male friends of, 55–56, 58,
   110–11, 130–32, 138–41, 164,
   190; see also Shakur,
   Lumumba; Shakur, Mutulu
as mother, 41, 47, 130, 135, 143,
   150–51, 154, 159–60, 162,
   184, 201
name of, 51, 55, 57–58
in New York, 30–36, 165–68, 169
origins of, 4–5, 11–13, 18–20,
   22–25, 49, 63, 64
parents of, see Williams, Rosa
   Belle; Williams, Walter Jr.
physical appearance of, 18, 28
on poverty, 15, 164
pregnancy of, 108, 109, 110–12,
   116, 118, 137–44

in prison, 57, 72, 87, 93, 94–95,
   104–7
qualities of, 16–17, 34–35,
   36–37, 79, 85, 86, 113–14,
   120–22, 151, 159, 164, 170,
   177, 185–86, 194, 203
as reader, 40–42, 65, 89, 203
rebirth of, 58–64, 173, 204–5
recovery of, 167–68, 169–78, 173,
   177, 179–83, 184–85
on resistance vs. revolution,
   14–15, 17, 78, 87–88
schooling of, 43–48, 127–28
self-acceptance of, 83
shootings by, 79, 84
sister of, see Cox, Glo
soul of an artist, 40
strength of, 58, 63, 77, 129, 131,
   191
on survival, 31–32, 65, 99, 129
trees planted by, 9, 10
trial of, 36, 49, 96–99, 103–4,
   108–12, 115–21
on trust, 50, 85, 87
and Tupac's business affairs,
   187–88, 189, 190, 191,
   193–99
on value, 130
voice of, 207–9
Shakur, Lumumba, 69–74, 76–86
   Afeni described by, 85–86
   Afeni's first husband, 69, 71–72,
      110–11, 121
   and collective biography, 85–86,
      90, 104
   debating with, 78, 81
   family of, 70, 81, 85
   first wife of, 81–82, 84, 85, 86,
      103–4, 121
   and Muslims, 71–72, 81, 86
   and Panthers, 71, 73, 76, 82,
      102–3, 121

Permissions

Manchild in the Promised Land © 1965 Claude Brown. By permission of the Estate of Claude Brown.

"Four Women" by Nina Simone © 1966 (Renewed) EMI Waterford Music, Inc and Rolles Royce Music Co. All rights for Rolles Royce Music Co. administered by EMI Waterford Music, Inc. All Rights Reserved. Used by permission Warner Bros. Publications U.S. Inc., Miami, 33014.

The Autobiography of Malcolm X © 1964 Alex Haley and Malcolm X, Ballantine Books, a division of Random House, Inc.

Lumumba Shakur excerpt from *Look for Me in the Whirlwind* copyright © 1971 by Lumumba Shakur. Used by permission of Random House, Inc.

Afeni Shakur excerpt from *Look for Me in the Whirlwind*